W9-COI-091

The Mexican-American War

by Don Nardo

America's
WARS

Lucent Books, P.O. Box 289011, San Diego, CA 92198-0011

Books in the America's Wars Series:

The Revolutionary War

The Indian Wars

The War of 1812

The Mexican-American War

The Civil War

The Spanish-American War

World War I

World War II: The War in the Pacific

World War II: The War in Europe

The Korean War

The Vietnam War

The Persian Gulf War

Library of Congress Cataloging-in-Publication Data

Nardo, Don, 1947–
    The Mexican-American War / by Don Nardo.
        p.   cm. — (America's wars series)
    Includes bibliographical references and index.
    Summary: Discusses the historical and cultural background of the
Mexican-American War and its major battles.
    ISBN 1-56006-402-1
    1. United States —History—War with Mexico, 1845–1848—Juvenile
literature.   [1. United States—History—War with Mexico,
1845–1848.] I. Title. II. Series.
E404.N37 1991
973.6'2—dc20   91–16728

Contents

Foreword

War, justifiable or not, is a descent into madness. George Washington, America's first president and commander-in-chief of its armed forces, wrote that his most fervent wish was "to see this plague of mankind, war, banished from the earth." Most, if not all of the forty presidents who succeeded Washington have echoed similar sentiments. Despite this, not one generation of Americans since the founding of the republic has been spared the maelstrom of war. In its brief history of just over two hundred years, the United States has been a combatant in eleven major wars. And four of those conflicts have occurred in the last fifty years.

America's reasons for going to war have differed little from those of most nations. Political, social, and economic forces were at work which either singly or in combination ushered America into each of its wars. A desire for independence motivated the Revolutionary War. The fear of annihilation led to the War of 1812. A related fear, that of having the nation divided, precipitated the Civil War. The need to contain an aggressor nation brought the United States into the Korean War. And territorial ambition lay behind the Mexican-American and the Indian Wars. Like all countries, America, at different times in its history, has been victimized by these forces and its citizens have been called to arms.

Whatever reasons may have been given to justify the use of military force, not all of America's wars have been popular. From the Revolutionary War to the Vietnam War, support of the people has alternately waxed and waned. For example, less than half of the colonists backed America's war of independence. In fact, most historians agree that at least one-third were committed to maintaining America's colonial status. During the Spanish-American War, a strong antiwar movement also developed. Resistance to the war was so high that the Democratic party made condemning the war a significant part of its platform in an attempt to lure voters into voting Democratic. The platform stated that "the burning issue of imperialism growing out of the Spanish war involves the very existence of the Republic and the destruction of our free institutions." More recently, the Vietnam War divided the nation like no other conflict had since the Civil War. The mushrooming antiwar movements in most major cities and colleges throughout the United States did more to bring that war to a conclusion than did actions on the battlefield.

Yet, there have been wars which have enjoyed overwhelming public support. World Wars I and II were popular because people believed that the survival of America's democratic institutions was at stake. In both wars, the American people rallied with an enthusiasm and spirit of self-sacrifice that was remarkable for a country with such a diverse population. Support for food and fuel rationing, the purchase of war bonds, a high rate of voluntary enlistments, and countless other forms of voluntarism, were characteristic of the people's response to those wars. Most recently, the Persian Gulf War prompted an unprecedented show of support even though the United States was not directly threatened by the conflict. Rallies in support of U.S. troops were widespread. Tens of thousands of individuals, including families, friends, and well-wishers of the troops sent packages of food, cosmetics, clothes, cassettes, and suntan oil. And even more supporters wrote letters to unknown soldiers that were forwarded to the military front. In fact, most public opinion polls revealed that up to 90 percent of all Americans approved of their nation's involvement.

The complex interplay of events and purposes that leads to military conflict should be included in a history of any war. A simple chronicling of battles and casualty lists at best offers only a partial history of war. Wars do not spontaneously erupt; nor does their memory perish. They are driven by underlying causes, fueled by policymakers, fought and supported by citizens, and remembered by those plotting a nation's future. For these reasons wars, or the fear of wars, will always leave an indelible stamp on any nation's history and influence its future.

The purpose of this series is to provide a full understanding of America's Wars by presenting each war in a historical context. Each of the twelve volumes focuses on the events that led up to the war, the war itself, its impact on the home front, and its aftermath and influence upon future conflicts. The unique personalities, the dramatic acts of courage and compassion, as well as the despair and horror of war are all presented in this series. Together, they show why America's wars have dominated American consciousness in the past as well as how they guide many political decisions of today. In these vivid and objective accounts, students will gain an understanding of why America became involved in these conflicts, and how historians, military and government officials, and others have come to understand and interpret that involvement.

Chronology of Events

1519–1521
Spanish adventurer Hernan Cortes conquers Central America, beginning centuries of Spanish rule.

1776
The American colonies adopt the Declaration of Independence while fighting to gain freedom from Great Britain.

1781
Revolutionary War ends.

1783
Treaty of Paris signed.

1803
The United States acquires the Louisiana Purchase from France.

1821
Mexican revolutionaries win self-rule from Spain. American Stephen Austin makes a deal with the Mexicans to allow American settlers in Texas.

1824
The Republic of Mexico is officially established.

1836
March 2 Texan patriots declare their independence, creating the Lone Star Republic.
March 6 Fall of the Alamo.
March 22 Texan garrison at Goliad executed by Mexicans.
April 21 Sam Houston defeats Mexicans at San Jacinto.

1844
James K. Polk elected president of the United States.

1845
The United States annexes Texas.

1846
May 8 Battle of Palo Alto.
May 13 The United States declares war on Mexico.
September 21–24 Battle of Monterrey.

Sam Houston, a former soldier and a renowned frontiersman, led the American resistance against Mexico in Texas.

1847
February 23 Battle of Buena Vista.
March 22–28 Bombardment and surrender of Vera Cruz.
April 18 Battle of Cerro Gordo.
September 13 Americans storm Chapultepec Hill in Mexico City.

1848
Treaty of Guadalupe Hidalgo signed, which ends the war.

INTRODUCTION

A Struggle for Land

For the United States, the first half of the nineteenth century was a period of swift and vigorous geographic expansion. Seeking money, land, and often adventure, tens of thousands of settlers left the eastern seaboard, crossed the Appalachian Mountains, and headed west into the American frontier. They cleared trees, planted crops, and built towns all through the forested valleys of Ohio, Tennessee, and Alabama. The young country's population grew quickly. Wave after wave of new pioneers surged into the undeveloped lands, pushing the border of American settlement ever westward.

U.S. desire for land led to American settlements in Texas and other parts of Mexico. Here, U.S. and Mexican troops battle near Mexico City.

Inevitably, this flood of American settlers reached the frontier region known as Texas. The sprawling, sparsely inhabited territory was an outlying province of the Republic of Mexico, which had recently gained its independence from Spain. During the 1820s and 1830s, thousands of homesteaders moved into Texas. They brought with them their American culture and a system of laws and political institutions that clashed with the Mexicans' way of life. The conflict eventually led the two nations to war.

For the Mexicans, the war was defensive. It was a fight to keep their lands and institutions. It was a struggle to protect their way of life from the aggressive and lawless "yanquis," a term the Mexicans used to refer to U.S. citizens.

The Americans were convinced it was their "manifest destiny" to expand across North America to the Pacific Ocean. Many said it was no accident that such vast, bountiful lands stretched before the youthful American nation. They proclaimed that God intended for Americans to settle these lands, including Texas.

The Mexican-American War from 1846 to 1848 was, more than anything else, a struggle for land. The victor would be able to claim the rolling plains of Texas, the rugged mountains of Colorado, and the fertile valleys of California. Both sides wanted to expand into and exploit this huge frontier. Both nations considered the land to be necessary space for supporting future, as well as existing, populations. In addition, the frontier offered an abundance of natural riches.

At the heart of the conflict between the two countries was a major difference of opinion about the nature of ownership. The Mexican government insisted that the land had long belonged to Mexico and therefore settlers had no right to make their homes on it. The American leaders believed the land belonged to anyone strong enough to take and hold it. It was a dispute that would be settled in blood.

CHAPTER ONE

Yanquis Overrun Texas— The Trouble Begins

The problems that led to the outbreak of the Mexican-American War grew out of several important cultural and political differences between the two nations. Although both the United States and Mexico were born out of revolutions against European powers, these European governments functioned quite differently and affected the way the two young countries developed.

Mexico gained its independence in the 1820s after a long and bloody revolution against Spain. The Mexican rebellion was inspired by the successful 1775 revolution in the United States and also by the French Revolution of 1789. By the early 1800s, many of the people of New Spain had become dissatisfied with Spanish rule. Inspired by the French and Americans, the Spanish colonists wanted to establish a democratic government with leaders elected by the people.

Among the most discontented of the colonists were the criollos (creoles), people of Spanish descent who had been born in the New World. The criollos deeply resented Spanish rule because they were granted less status and power than the pure Spanish *grachupines.* The *grachupines* had been born in Spain, held almost all of the important and powerful offices, and received constant favors from the Spanish king and the viceroy, the local leader. The criollos thought that if New Spain were to break away from Spanish rule, the *grachupines* would no longer prevent them from gaining power.

Another group that wanted to break away from Spain consisted of the mestizos, the offspring of mixed marriages between

An American militiaman hangs the Stars and Stripes in this 1783 lithograph, symbolizing the birth of American independence.

Spanish colonists and local Indians. Those in power considered the mestizos, as well as the Indians themselves, to be racially inferior. Members of both groups were mainly poor laborers who worked long hours in the fields and mines for low wages. They lived in primitive huts made of adobe, sun-dried bricks of clay or straw. These people had little or no say in choosing their own leaders and no chance of rising out of poverty. Many mestizos, demanding fair treatment under the law, joined forces with the rebellious criollos.

After several bloody rebellions over an eleven-year period, criollo and mestizo revolutionaries in New Spain gained self-rule in 1821. They formally established the Republic of Mexico in 1824.

The newly established country of Mexico inherited all of the lands of the former colony. It was a vast territory covering more than one million square miles. The steaming equatorial jungles of Panama formed the southern border, while the northernmost reaches touched the great level plains of Kansas and the snow-capped peaks of Colorado. In between stretched all manner of terrains and climates: the blistering deserts of New Mexico and Arizona; the lush, nearly impenetrable rain forests of the Yucatan Peninsula; and the fertile farmlands and fine natural harbors of California.

Vincente Guerrero (center), shown in this 1819 lithograph, was a Mexican revolutionary.

Mexico Under the Spanish

The Spanish soldier-adventurer Hernan Cortes conquered Mexico between 1519 and 1521. Because the Spanish possessed gunpowder, cannons, and other advanced weaponry, they easily defeated the Aztecs, Mayans, and other local Indian nations. From that time until Mexico achieved self-rule in 1821, the Spanish controlled this colony known as New Spain.

The Spanish, like most other Europeans of the time, believed that European culture was superior to the cultures of other, more primitive peoples. So, the Spanish imposed their own customs, language, and religion on the Indians of Central America. At first, the natives tried to resist these new ways. But as time passed, many marriages occurred between the Spanish and Indians, resulting in a mixed racial group known as the mestizos. The mestizos learned that adopting Spanish culture brought them improved social status and better treatment by the ruling Spanish elite. Even after the 1821 revolution, Indians and mestizos found it necessary to conform to Spanish ways.

All official business and communication in New Spain was conducted in Spanish. Although more than fifty native languages continued to flourish in the country, most Indians and all mestizos learned to speak Spanish out of necessity. Similarly, Spanish laws, marriage customs, clothing, military traditions, and music predominated in the colony.

One of the most important aspects of Spanish culture was religion. The Spanish believed that it was their duty to God to convert other peoples to Catholicism. No other religions were permitted in New Spain. In fact, the practice of other faiths, or even public criticism of Catholicism, constituted heresy, the crime of expressing opinions contrary to Catholic teachings. Heresy was punishable by imprisonment or

Spanish troops led by soldier-adventurer Hernan Cortes conquered Mexico around 1520.

death. The influence of Spanish Catholicism in Mexican culture was so strong that even in the twentieth century, when other faiths were allowed to exist in Mexico, more than 97 percent of the population remained Catholic.

The Mexican Revolution of 1821

The 1775 American and 1789 French revolutions significantly affected the people of New Spain. Ideas about equality and self-rule began to influence the Spanish colonists. In the early 1800s, the criollos, those born in Mexico of Spanish descent, sought to share power with the ruling *grachupines*, those born in Spain. A few radical criollos, however, wanted to throw out the *grachupines* and declare the colony an independent country.

Several rebellions occurred, the first in 1810. On September 16, a large group of mestizos, led by a priest named Miguel Hidalgo, marched on Mexico City. The *grachupines* quickly crushed the uprising and executed Hidalgo. But the incident inspired many Mexicans to continue the struggle for freedom. The martyred Hidalgo became a popular folk hero, and September 16 is still celebrated as Mexico's Independence Day.

In 1813 and 1814, a better-organized rebellion, this one led by Hidalgo's pupil Jose Maria Morelos, succeeded in winning control of most of southern Mexico. But this uprising also failed, and like Hidalgo, Morelos was captured and put to death. Despite these setbacks, the revolutionary movement continued.

Finally, in 1821, a group of clergymen and important criollos who favored self-rule joined forces with the rebels. Led by Augustin de Iturbide, a wealthy criollo landowner, they convinced almost every powerful leader in the colony to join them. Under tremendous pressure, the viceroy granted Mexican independence in August 1821.

At first, only the congress was elected by the people. Iturbide took power as president and later declared himself emperor. Deciding that this was no better than being ruled by the Spanish king, military leaders removed Iturbide from power in 1823 and eventually executed him.

In 1824, the Mexican congress established the Republic of Mexico, adopting a constitution similar to that of the United States. The leaders divided Mexico into nineteen states and four territories, and the people elected Guadalupe Victoria as their first president.

Hidalgo (left) and Morelos (center) both fought for Mexican independence. They were executed for their efforts. Ironically, Iturbide (right), who became president after Mexico achieved independence, was executed for exceeding his powers.

Mexico's New Government

The administration of these lands was now in the hands of Mexico's new government. Like the United States, Mexico had an elected president and legislature. It also had a constitution patterned after that of the United States. Mexico, however, maintained an official state religion, while the United States did not. All Mexican citizens were expected to follow the teachings of Catholicism, the religion introduced many years before by the Spanish.

Although the new country had established a democratic form of government, most of the former class differences among its citizens remained. The *grachupines* were still wealthy and influential, although many more criollos now attained positions of political power. Some mestizos received better treatment and opportunities, but many remained poor, second-class citizens. With few exceptions, the Indians continued to be treated as inferior.

One of the main reasons Mexican society remained divided between those with money and social status and those without was due to its Spanish traditions. Spain was a monarchy in which the king had the final say in all government matters. So even after Mexico gained its independence and established a democratic form of government, its traditions were rooted in monarchies. This tradition was so strong that it was often easy for dictators to seize absolute power and enforce their will on the people.

Like Mexico, the United States had its extremes of wealth and poverty. But the country's founders had created a system in which the poorest and least educated could, through hard work, rise to positions of power and influence. As Thomas Jefferson wrote in the Declaration of Independence, "We hold these truths to be self-evident, that all men are created equal."

Equality for All People

Unlike Mexico, the United States was founded on the ideal of equality for all people. The United States also adopted the democratic traditions of its mother country, England. Even though England was, like Spain, a monarchy, it also had a parliament, a governing body made up of representatives elected by the people. In many ways, Parliament had more power than the king and made many of the important national decisions. England provided a heritage of democratic traditions that the United States expanded upon and embodied in its own laws and government procedures.

But the young United States did not achieve its goal of true equality. Slavery still existed in the United States even after the Revolution. The issue of slavery sharply divided many Americans into opposing camps, even in the nation's earliest years. Those

The founding fathers (right) revered the democratic traditions of England followed by King George III (left). Mexico's governmental tradition, however, was more firmly rooted in monarchy and wealth. This was one difference between Mexico and the United States.

who accepted or supported slavery interpreted Jefferson's phrase "all men" to refer mainly to white people of European ancestry. Slaveholders often regarded blacks and other nonwhites as less than human. Some owners treated their slaves like animals and severely beat them if they misbehaved. Slaves were also often considered to be childlike and mentally inferior to their masters. Most slavery supporters agreed that slaves were not the equals of whites and that slavery was therefore justified.

Those against slavery believed that all people should be respected, regardless of race or ancestry. They focused on the similarities of all humans rather than on the differences of race and social status. Opponents of slavery argued for a literal interpretation of Jefferson's words. Eventually, bitter disagreements over slavery would lead the United States into a bloody civil war.

The Fledgling Nation

Because of the existence of slavery, some Americans did not enjoy the benefits of equality and justice. Yet the official adoption of such ideals had a profound effect on the fledgling nation. A majority of Americans came to believe that all citizens should enjoy equal access to social and political opportunities. Those who worked the hardest to take advantage of these opportunities would become the most successful. This idea established a society in which people would be judged primarily by their personal achievements. By contrast, in Mexico, despite the new democratic constitution, people still tended to judge one another according to wealth and social status.

American ideals of freedom and equality also ensured that people could worship any god any way they wanted, without interference from the government. Although most Americans were Protestants, the Constitution dictated that government and religion be kept completely separate. Many Mexicans misinterpreted the American separation of church and state as an expression of contempt for religion. The Mexicans developed a popular stereotype of Americans as anti-Catholic ruffians bent upon destroying the church. This stereotype would later fuel bitter anti-American feelings among Mexicans during the conflict between the two nations.

In addition to American ideas about freedom and religion, geography also played a part in shaping the early United States. The early United States covered a great deal of territory. The young country held authority over lands stretching from the Atlantic Ocean to the Mississippi River. But, at first, most American settlement was confined to the narrow coastal strip between the ocean and the Appalachian Mountains. For many years, the United States and Mexico were separated by large tracts of undeveloped territory inhabited by only a few widely spaced Indian tribes. As a result, there was little contact between the two countries.

While America's Southern states permitted slavery, Mexico firmly opposed it. In these nineteenth-century lithographs, a slave (left) is seen escaping from a Southern plantation. The metal brace around his neck is heavy and pronged, making running difficult. A slave trader (below, far right) inspects slaves in New Orleans.

This situation began to change in the early nineteenth century as the United States rapidly expanded westward. The federal government's 1803 purchase of the Louisiana Territory from France nearly doubled the size of the United States. By 1819, the country had added eight new states as well as the Arkansas and Missouri territories, which bordered directly on Mexico. With these areas now available, American settlers began to move into them, and from there, they began to enter illegally the sparsely inhabited Mexican territories of California, New Mexico, and Texas. At that time, Mexico was involved in its war for independence from Spain. Authorities in Mexico City were forced to ignore the troublesome intruders in their outlying provinces.

Once the Mexican republic was firmly established, however, the new regime turned its attention to its borders. It looked upon the expanding United States as a threat. Mexican leaders feared that the Americans would use the yanqui settlements in Texas as an excuse to seize that Mexican province.

A Proposal by Austin

In 1821, a young American law student named Stephen Austin offered the Mexicans a deal that appeared to solve the problem of American settlers in Texas. Austin asked the Mexican government for permission to settle Anglos, or white Americans, in Texas. Austin promised that the settlers would give up allegiance to the United States and become Mexican citizens. They would also convert to Catholicism and obey Mexican laws. Gaining Mexican citizens and increasing the population of Texas were ideas that appealed to the Mexican leaders. In this way, the Mexicans could set up a buffer zone, an area well-populated by loyal Mexican citizens, between itself and the United States. The Mexicans agreed to Austin's requests.

But the hordes of settlers that poured into Texas in the 1820s did not live up to their side of the bargain. For one thing, they refused to become Catholics. As Americans, they were used to the idea of freedom of religion and resented being told how to worship.

Slavery proved to be another problem. Many of the settlers came from southern states and brought their slaves with them into Texas. Slavery did not exist in Mexico, and Mexican leaders objected. When the settlers ignored the objections, Mexico officially outlawed slavery in Texas in 1829. Many Texans ignored the decree and kept their slaves.

As more and more Americans entered Texas and ignored Mexican laws, Mexican leaders decided that the situation was getting out of control. The government in Mexico City established immigration laws to regulate the number of settlers entering Texas. The Texans ignored these laws, too.

Stephen Austin and the Texas Deal

Stephen F. Austin (1793–1836) was one of the principal figures in early Mexican-American relations. Austin was drawn to Texas because of his father, Moses Austin, a frontier businessman and colonizer. In January 1821, the elder Austin convinced the viceroy of New Spain to grant 200,000 acres in Texas for colonization by American settlers. Only six months later, he died, and Stephen, then a young law student in New Orleans, hurried to Texas to carry on his father's work.

For the next fourteen years, Austin successfully negotiated many land deals with the Mexican government. He argued that Texas was nearly uninhabited, undeveloped, and therefore useless to Mexico. He proposed that Anglo settlements would increase the value of the land and bring Mexico needed tax revenues. Mexico agreed to open up Texas for colonization under specific conditions. The settlers would have to become Mexican citizens, obey Mexican laws, and convert to Catholicism. In order to own land in Texas, thousands of settlers agreed to these conditions.

Although Austin himself dealt with the Mexicans in good faith, many of the American settlers later refused to follow the terms of the agreement. Most refused to become Catholics and openly broke many Mexican laws. This led to increased tensions and eventually armed conflict between the Mexicans and Anglos. Angry Mexican officials imprisoned Austin in 1833 but released him two years later. He died shortly afterward at the age of forty-three, surviving just long enough to see Texas declare its independence. An independent Texas had not been his original goal, but when it came, he was pleased.

Stephen Austin, a lawyer, helped establish American colonies in Texas.

Frustrations Mount

Believing that the Texans were Mexican citizens who should obey Mexican laws, Mexican leaders became increasingly frustrated. But for years, the Mexicans did little to enforce these laws in Texas, due partly to the instability of the Mexican government. Leaders rose and fell frequently. The great distance between Texas and Mexico City was another reason that the Mexicans did not properly enforce their laws in Texas. Most of the Texan settlements were located nearly eight hundred miles north of Mexico City. The journey across rugged mountains, deserts, and more than a dozen rivers was both difficult and time-consuming for Mexican officials.

By 1834, more than thirty thousand former Americans lived in Texas. Native Mexicans in the province, mostly mestizos tending small farms or cattle ranches, numbered about seventy-five hundred. The two groups had very different attitudes about homesteading in Texas and frequently disagreed. The local Mexicans resented the Anglos for bringing slaves to Texas and also for purposely disobeying Mexican laws. The Mexicans were contented to follow the dictates of whatever leader happened to be in power in Mexico City.

In this 1822 lithograph, Stephen Austin issues a land title to colonists in Texas. The title allowed colonists to homestead land.

By contrast, the American Texans tended to be fiercely independent. Many shunned local Mexican customs and felt they did not have to follow Mexican laws. Some openly admitted that they had taken the oath of allegiance to Mexico only to get homesteads and had no intention of becoming loyal Mexican citizens. Many Anglos, especially slave owners, looked down on the racially mixed mestizos as inferiors and often treated them with disrespect.

Gun Battles Begin

As tensions rose in Texas, fights erupted between individual Mexicans and Anglos. A few incidents escalated into gun battles, and several people on both sides were wounded. Worried officials in Mexico City began to believe rumors that the U.S. government had purposely organized the settlers in an attempt to take over Texas. The rumors were never verified, but fearful Mexican officials imposed new and tighter restrictions on Anglos in Texas.

The most controversial of these restrictions stated that anyone entering or living in Texas with an unregistered gun would be considered a pirate and subject to immediate execution. This greatly angered the Texan Anglos. Almost every American in Texas owned a gun for protection against Indians, and most of these weapons were not registered. Believing that the government had no business regulating their guns, few Anglos complied with the law. They viewed it as a direct attack on their personal freedoms and vowed to fight if the law were actually enforced.

Santa Anna Emerges

Late in 1834, an event occurred that increased tensions in the region even more. Gen. Antonio Lopez de Santa Anna, supreme commander of the Mexican army, made himself dictator of Mexico. He believed that the former leaders had not been strict enough with the Texans. In 1835, he sent troops to reinforce several small Mexican garrisons, or groups of soldiers at military outposts, near the mighty Rio Grande in southern Texas. He felt confident that this show of force would discourage the Texans from breaking any more laws.

But Santa Anna's strategy backfired. At the sight of the troops, Texan tempers flared. Gangs of angry Anglos fired on Mexican patrols, and the Mexicans fired back. As hostilities quickly escalated, the Texans organized a formal resistance group. This armed militia boldly attacked and took control of the towns of Gonzales and San Antonio. The Texans hoped this would send a signal to Santa Anna that they would not be intimidated by threats.

Americans Who Settled Texas

Most of the American settlers who ended up in Texas sought land on which to start new lives as farmers or ranchers. They were independent, rugged individuals accustomed to taking care of themselves in primitive areas of the American frontier. Such areas were far from government authorities, and the settlers were used to making and enforcing their own rules. In time, they became suspicious of big government, believing that they knew best how to manage their own affairs. Frontier life had given them a special kind of freedom from authority that they cherished.

This stubborn attitude persisted after the settlers moved into the Texan frontier. They were willing to swear allegiance to Mexico in order to get land, but they resented being told what to do by Mexican authorities. The settlers objected to many unfamiliar Mexican laws and social customs. They especially disliked the idea of being forced to become Catholics simply because Catholicism was Mexico's state religion. As the Mexicans applied more and more pressure, the former Americans felt their freedom threatened. Eventually, they concluded that armed resistance was the only way to defend their way of life.

Gen. Antonio Lopez de Santa Anna, dictator of Mexico, sent troops to suppress the rowdy Texan revolts. The Texans retaliated against Mexican troops by taking the towns of Gonzales and San Antonio.

When news of these events reached Mexico City, Santa Anna was furious. His high-ranking officers as well as several top government officials agreed that the Texan attacks constituted armed rebellion. They concluded that the Anglos in Texas needed to be taught a lesson once and for all.

Early in 1836, Santa Anna assembled six thousand seasoned troops, along with dozens of heavy cannons, siege equipment, and hundreds of tons of supplies. He had two goals. First, he would march the troops to Texas and crush the Anglo resistance. More important, he would send a warning signal to the U.S. government, which he believed was behind all the trouble. Shortly before leaving Mexico City, he boasted to the British ambassador, "If the yanquis interfere when I put down the revolt, I will annihilate them and plant the Mexican flag in Washington, D.C." To the sounds of flutes and drums, the soldiers, clad in neatly pressed uniforms of green and white, marched out of the city and north toward the Rio Grande.

CHAPTER TWO

Victory or Death – Texas Declares Its Independence

News of the approach of Santa Anna's army spread like a prairie fire through Texas. In February 1836, Texan scouts brought news of enemy troops to the leaders of the Texas resistance. The approaching army was large, they said, and well-equipped. The Mexicans would reach the Rio Grande in southern Texas in one month or less, which left very little time for the resistance to organize a defense.

The Texans had no organized, official army. Their forces consisted of only a few hundred men, armed mainly with rifles, divided into several tiny garrisons. One was located in the small village of San Antonio, about 150 miles northeast of the Rio Grande. There were other Texan outposts in the cities of Gonzales, about 60 miles east of San Antonio, and Goliad, 80 miles to the south.

Sam Houston Leads the Resistance

The Texans recognized Sam Houston as the leader of the resistance. He was a former soldier and a renowned frontiersman and had served once as governor of Tennessee. Houston realized that although the Texans were angry and ready to fight, they were also poorly organized and spread out over thousands of square miles. His first priority was to organize the scattered settlers into a fighting force that would have a chance against Santa Anna's well-trained troops. This would take time. Meanwhile, the small garrisons at San Antonio and other villages would have to hold out as best and as long as they could against the approaching enemy.

Sam Houston, a former soldier and frontiersman, led the Texas revolt.

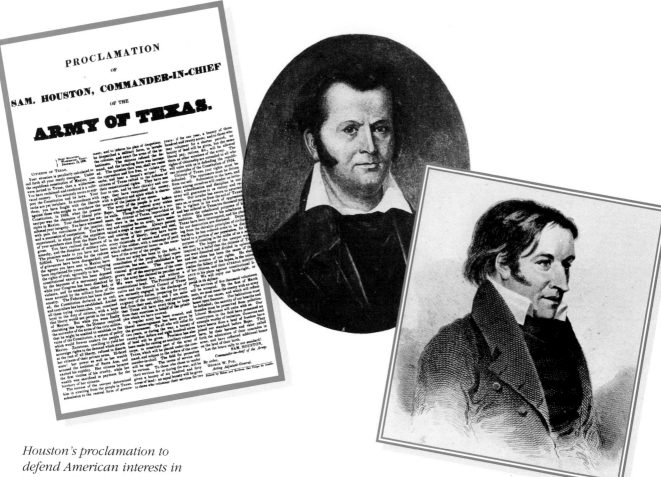

Houston's proclamation to defend American interests in Texas (left) led men like Jim Bowie (center) and Davy Crockett (right) to join rebel Texans against Mexico.

Preparing for War

In a hurried attempt to prepare for the Mexican onslaught, Texans with former military training took charge of the garrisons. In February 1836, Col. William Barrett Travis and famed frontiersman Jim Bowie assumed command of the tiny militia at the San Antonio garrison. The garrison consisted of fewer than 100 men. Luckily, a few new recruits arrived each day, and by February 22, the size of the force had increased to 150.

Most of the new arrivals were volunteers from nearby states. Some of these were frontiersmen looking for adventure, or just a good fight. Among them was the legendary Indian fighter and former U.S. congressman Davy Crockett. Other volunteers were settlers looking for land. They gambled that the Texans would win the fight, then grant them free homesteads.

Travis and Bowie welcomed the new recruits and immediately put them to work stockpiling provisions and preparing fortifications. Believing Santa Anna still to be many days away, Travis and Bowie were confident that their defenses would be ready when the Mexicans arrived.

Davy Crockett—Hero of the Alamo

Born in a pioneer cabin in eastern Tennessee in 1786, Davy Crockett became a legendary figure of the early American frontier. It is sometimes difficult to separate his real deeds from the fantastic exploits depicted in books and movies. Several of the most popular stories about him were complete fabrications. For instance, he did not stare down, then wrestle and subdue full-grown grizzly bears.

Still, the real Davy Crockett was a highly colorful person who lived a life of unusual accomplishment and adventure. He often wore a coonskin cap and affectionately called his favorite rifle Betsy. He was also an expert fiddle player and carried his instrument wherever he went.

Crockett said he wanted to be "where the action is" whenever possible. He eagerly volunteered to fight in the Creek Indian wars in Tennessee from 1813 to 1815. It was here that he earned his reputation as an Indian fighter and met future president Andrew Jackson. When peace returned to the frontier, he decided to look for action in the political arena. In 1821, he won a seat in the Tennessee legislature, where he sometimes wore backwoods clothes made of buckskin to gain attention. He became a skilled politician, serving three terms in Congress. There, he often opposed the policies of his old friend, Andrew Jackson, another politician with a frontier image.

In 1835, Crockett ran for Congress again but lost. Restless, he set his sights on Texas, where fighting had already erupted between Anglo settlers and Mexican troops. Wearing his buckskins and carrying Betsy and his fiddle, he set out on foot from Tennessee, reaching San Antonio in February 1836. There, he offered his

Davy Crockett was a legendary woodsman and Indian fighter. After three terms as a U.S. congressman, he went to Texas to help fight Mexican troops.

services to Colonel Travis. Reportedly, Crockett's first words on arrival were, "Where's the action?" He died fighting with the other Alamo defenders on March 6, 1836, adding a fitting final chapter to his legacy as a frontier hero.

Meanwhile, Col. James W. Fannin, another Texan with former U.S. military training, took charge of the garrison at Goliad. Most of the 350 American volunteers under Fannin's command were new to Texas, having arrived recently from the United States. All had entered Texas carrying firearms. They knew full well that this branded them as pirates and that they could be shot on sight. But they came anyway. Like so many other American volunteers, they believed the chance for free land was worth the risk. In addition, there were rumors that the Mexican army was hundreds of miles away and that they would probably never see any real action. Most of the volunteers, young and inexperienced in warfare, believed the rumors.

But the Mexican forces were not as far away as the volunteers and their commanders hoped. The tough, glory-seeking Santa Anna marched his men at an impossible pace and reached the Alazan River, only a few miles north of San Antonio, by the morning of February 23, 1836.

Travis ordered that the town's church bells be rung to alert and assemble the garrison. At the same time, one of Travis's scouts galloped up and reported the approach of the Mexican vanguard, the military units traveling ahead of the army's main body. The vanguard, numbering at least six hundred men and carrying several cannons, was eight miles away and closing fast. There was no time to complete the defenses in the town. So Travis ordered the garrison to move into the Alamo, an old abandoned Spanish monastery on the outskirts of town. Bowie, stricken a few days before with pneumonia, had to be carried on a stretcher. Once inside the Alamo, Travis made preparations for

With no time to prepare the defense of San Antonio against Mexican attack, Col. William Barrett Travis (above) ordered his garrison to move into the Alamo (right) on the outskirts of town.

This nineteenth-century lithograph shows the siege of the Alamo on March 6, 1836. The final attack occurred after the Mexican army barraged the fort with continuous cannon fire for thirteen days.

battle. He sent a messenger to ask Sam Houston for reinforcements, though he knew there was little chance of help arriving in time. He had his soldiers drag in about thirty cannons captured during the taking of the town. But supplies of gunpowder were low, so many of the big guns were useless. Realizing they would no longer be able to get water from a nearby river, Travis ordered his men to dig a well inside the mission walls.

That day, the Mexican vanguard reclaimed the town and prepared for the arrival of Santa Anna and the rest of the army. The vanguard commander hoped to save lives on both sides by avoiding a fight. He sent a messenger with a white flag to offer Travis a deal. The Mexicans would spare the Texans' lives if the defenders surrendered their arms and agreed to swear loyalty to Mexico.

No Deals

As the messenger approached the Alamo, the Texans suddenly fired a cannon, narrowly missing him. Travis wanted to make it clear to the Mexicans that the Texans were not interested in making deals or even in talking. Firing the cannon sent a message to the enemy: either go back to Mexico or prepare to fight. This act horrified the Mexicans, for firing on a white flag was considered a barbaric act. The Mexican commander angrily ordered his men to raise a red flag high enough for the Texans to see. He also called for the buglers to sound the dreaded bugle call known as the *deguello*. Both of these gestures meant that the Mexicans would show no mercy. It would be a fight to the death.

Weapons of the Alamo Siege

The arms used by both Texans and Mexicans at the Alamo were the most common weapons in use in the early nineteenth century. The most powerful of these were the cannons, which had a range of hundreds of yards and could easily batter down stone walls. The various kinds of cannons were designated by the weights of the cannonballs they fired. For example, a cannon that fired an eight-pound ball was called an "eight-pounder." Most of the cannons used in the Alamo siege were eight-, ten-, or twelve-pounders. Each fighting man carried a flintlock, or musket, a primitive rifle invented by the Spanish in the 1500s. A soldier loaded the weapon by pouring gunpowder down the front barrel, then inserting a lead ball. Pulling the trigger caused a metal hammer to strike a piece of flint, producing a spark. This ignited the powder, which blasted the ball out of the barrel. Flintlocks could fire up to two hundred yards, but they took a long time to load and were not very accurate.

Other weapons of the time included razor-sharp swords and bayonets for hand-to-hand fighting. Many Americans preferred bowie knives, made popular by frontiersman Jim Bowie, because of their unusually large, curved blades. There were also lances, or pikes, long spears carried by horsemen. These soldiers, appropriately called lancers or pikemen, were descendants of medieval jousting knights. Mounted lancers proved most effective when skewering retreating foot soldiers.

Fighters used various weapons during the Alamo battle, including the Texas Army flintlock pistol (right) and the flintlock rifle (below). A flintlock is any firearm that uses a flint to ignite gunpowder.

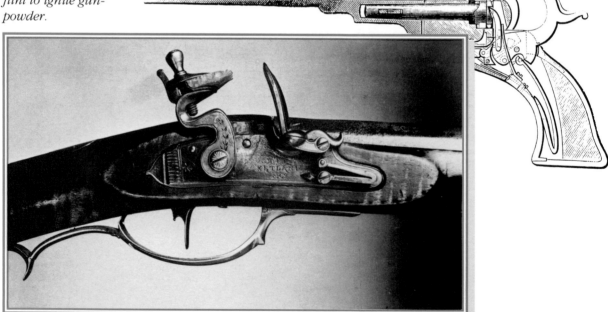

In the battle of the Alamo, Mexican and Texan troops relied on cannon (above), muskets (center), and knives (below). The knife and scabbard shown here belonged to Jim Bowie.

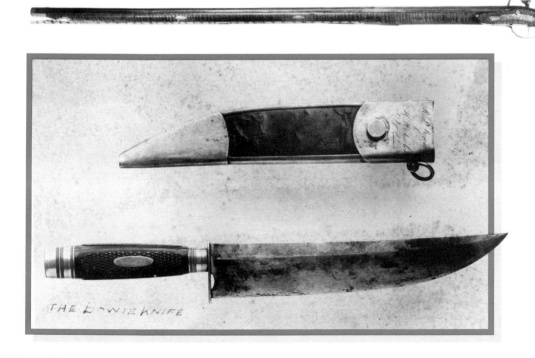

THE BOWIE KNIFE

Colonel Travis reviews troops at the Alamo shortly before the fighting begins.

About an hour later, the Mexican cannons began firing. They continued the rest of the day and on through the night. The next morning, as units of the Mexican army began to surround the Alamo, Travis wrote the following message:

> To the people of Texas & all Americans in the world: Fellow Citizens and Compatriots—I am besieged by a thousand or more of the Mexicans under Santa Anna—I have sustained a continued bombardment and cannonade for 24 hours and have not lost a man…our flag still waves proudly from the walls—*I shall never surrender or retreat*. Then, I call upon you in the name of liberty, of patriotism, and everything dear to the American character, to come to our aid, with all dispatch…. I am determined to sustain myself as long as possible and die like a soldier who never forgets what is due to his honor and that of his country—Victory or Death.

That evening, a Texan boy managed to carry the message through the Mexican lines and rode at top speed toward Sam Houston's camp many miles to the north.

A few days later, the Alamo defenders saw banners unfurled and heard trumpet volleys in San Antonio. Santa Anna had arrived. The general assessed the situation, ordered the cannon barrage to continue, and began preparations for an assault on the Alamo. Confident of an easy victory, Santa Anna claimed to be in a good mood. But his satisfaction turned to rage on the night of March 1, when his sentries allowed a band of Texan reinforcements to slip through the Mexican lines. Thirty-two volunteers from nearby Gonzales made it into the Alamo. This increased the number of defenders to 187, including Bowie and several other sick men.

Attack the Alamo!

Early in the bleak, overcast morning of March 6, 1836, after thirteen days of almost continuous cannon barrage, Santa Anna ordered an all-out attack on the Alamo. The Mexicans executed the assault with perfect military precision. They charged the mission from all sides at once, using scaling ladders to reach the tops of the walls. Though the defenders fought valiantly, they were quickly overwhelmed by the great numbers of Mexican soldiers.

Waves of Mexicans climbed over the walls and poured into the courtyard of the mission. They shot Travis as he was trying to load a cannon. A minute later, Davy Crockett ran out of powder and used his famous rifle named Betsy as a club. He managed to kill more than a dozen of the Mexicans before they cut him down with swords. Bowie was still in bed when the attackers

Davy Crockett was a rugged frontiersman, as this woodcut portrays (above). His death at the Alamo (right) ensured his legendary fame in American history.

broke into the makeshift hospital. He drew the notorious knife he had designed (known as a bowie knife) and managed to wound a few of them as they slashed him with their bayonets. Near the end of the battle, about twenty of the defenders slipped over a wall and tried to get away. But Santa Anna had anticipated such a move, and his mounted soldiers armed with lances, or spears, killed the escaping Texans.

In less than thirty minutes, all 187 of the Alamo defenders were dead. But they had managed to kill more than 1,500 Mexicans during the siege and final battle. As a gesture of revenge, the enraged Santa Anna refused to give the dead Texans a proper burial. His soldiers stripped the Texan bodies, then piled them together and burned them.

An Independent State

Santa Anna did not know that during the last days of the Alamo siege, a fateful meeting had convened more than one hundred miles to the north. On March 2, 1836, in the tiny village of Washington-on-the-Brazos, fifty-nine leaders of the Texas resistance declared Texas to be independent, and the Lone Star Republic was formed. They elected David G. Burnet provisional, or temporary, president and placed Sam Houston in command of the army.

After the meeting, Houston, who had already received Travis's plea for help, hastily organized reinforcements. It was not until March 10, four days after the Alamo was lost, that Houston learned of the tragedy. He immediately sent orders telling Fannin and the garrison at Goliad to retreat. By the time Fannin received the message and organized the retreat, however, it was March 19. Fannin marched his men out of the town early that morning, but less than two hours later, a large Mexican force overtook them.

Led by General Urrea, Santa Anna's right-hand man, the Mexicans numbered more than one thousand, including both cavalry, or troops mounted on horses, and well-armed infantry. The disciplined Mexican troops moved quickly. Before Fannin could order a return to Goliad, they surrounded his men in an open field and attacked. After a few minutes of fighting, Urrea pulled his men back and regrouped them. Though the brief battle was indecisive, more than sixty Texans were wounded and the situation appeared hopeless. The next day, Fannin raised a white flag and ordered his men to surrender their guns.

Open Defiance

The Mexicans marched the Texans back to Goliad and locked them in the local church. One week later, on March 27, the morning of Palm Sunday, guards awakened the prisoners and led them about one mile out of town. There, the Mexicans carried

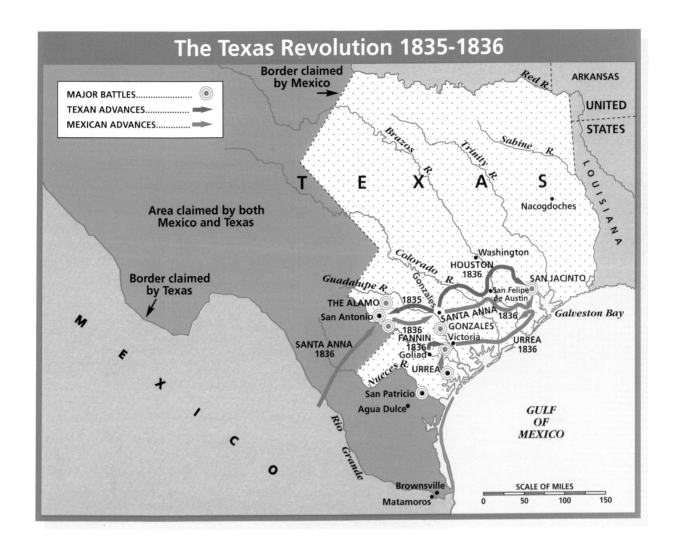

The Texas Revolution 1835-1836

MAJOR BATTLES.................... ◉
TEXAN ADVANCES................. ➤
MEXICAN ADVANCES............. ➤

Border claimed by Mexico →

ARKANSAS

UNITED STATES

LOUISIANA

Red R.

Sabine R.

Trinity R.

Brazos R.

T E X A S

Nacogdoches

Washington
HOUSTON
1836
SAN JACINTO

Colorado R.
Gonzales
San Felipe de Austin
Guadalupe R.

Area claimed by both Mexico and Texas

Border claimed by Texas ↓

M E X I C O

THE ALAMO ◉ 1835
San Antonio ●
SANTA ANNA 1836
1836
FANNIN
1836
Goliad ●
GONZALES ◉
Victoria ●
SANTA ANNA 1836 ◉
Galveston Bay
URREA
1836

Nueces R. URREA ◉

San Patricio ◉
Agua Dulce ●

GULF OF MEXICO

Rio Grande

Brownsville ●
Matamoros ●

SCALE OF MILES
0   50   100   150

out orders from Santa Anna, who was camped with his army about one hundred miles away. A column of Mexican soldiers lined up the Texans and shot them. There was no trial, which was standard procedure for prisoners of war. The execution was justified, according to Santa Anna, because the Texans were pirates who had openly defied Mexican law.

Other Texans did not share Santa Anna's view. They said his troops had committed murder. And when news of the massacre reached the United States about one week later, many Americans were outraged. Because those who had died at the Alamo and Goliad were Americans or former Americans, public opinion predictably sympathized with the Texans.

Sam Houston used the Alamo and Goliad tragedies to build up anti-Mexican sentiment. He called upon all Texans to remember the sacrifice of their countrymen and to join the fight against the Mexican "invaders." Within two weeks, his ragtag army of 450 had grown to more than 800. During the first half of April,

The Deaths at Goliad

On March 19, 1836, Col. James W. Fannin marched his 350-man garrison out of the town of Goliad in eastern Texas. He had orders from Sam Houston to retreat before Santa Anna's superior forces, which had captured the Alamo only days before. Shortly after the Texans left Goliad, a large force of Mexicans led by General Urrea overtook them. The troops engaged in a savage pitched battle. Fannin's group suffered heavy casualties. Believing that his men would be treated as prisoners of war, Fannin surrendered and the Mexicans imprisoned the Texans in the church in Goliad.

The next day, General Urrea departed, leaving Colonel Portilla in charge. One week later, Portilla received a message from Santa Anna, claiming that the prisoners had entered Mexican territory carrying guns in defiance of Mexican law. They were pirates and were to be shot immediately. Portilla and his fellow officers believed the orders drastic and inhumane. They agonized all night over whether or not to follow them. Finally deciding that Santa Anna would have them shot if they disobeyed, they reluctantly carried out the mass execution.

The incident created an instant controversy. To Americans, Fannin and his men were heroes, martyrs to the cause of freedom. They had clearly been gunned down in cold blood. The Mexican government saw things differently. It defended Santa Anna's actions, insisting that the prisoners were pirates who had threatened the peace of the republic. Many Americans and Mexicans still hold these opposing views of the event.

Colonel Portilla (left) of the Mexican army reluctantly carried out orders given by General Santa Anna to kill 350 Texan soldiers led by Col. James W. Fannin. A monument to Fannin's men stands today in Goliad (above).

Houston repeatedly ordered his men to fall back before Santa Anna's army, which moved from town to town, seizing Texan supplies and burning buildings. It was clear that the Mexican general was trying to destroy all means of support for the Texan rebels. Houston's strategy was to wait for Santa Anna to make a mistake. He needed Santa Anna to let his guard down long enough to give the much smaller Texan forces the advantage.

Santa Anna's Mistake

On April 21, 1836, the two armies camped about one mile from each other on the banks of the San Jacinto River about 180 miles east of San Antonio. This spot would later become the site of the city of Houston. Santa Anna believed that the Texans, inferior in number and training, would not dare to attack his camp. So he erected no stockade barriers and posted few sentries. This was the mistake Houston had been waiting for.

At 3:30 in the afternoon, while the Mexicans rested during their customary siesta, or nap, Houston's men suddenly burst forth from the cover of some oak trees and descended upon the

This Norman Price painting Remember Goliad *shows a line of Mexican soldiers firing upon the defenseless Texan prisoners of war.*

Gen. Antonio Lopez de Santa Anna

For nearly half a century, Santa Anna (1794–1876) was the most dominant figure in Mexican politics and military affairs. He ruled his country as president or dictator eleven times between 1833 and 1855. Only rarely was he elected by the people. Usually, he used his army to seize power, proclaim himself dictator, and throw out the country's constitution. Yet even as a dictator, many Mexicans supported him. After centuries of Spanish rule, the Mexican people were accustomed to tough, authoritarian leadership. They saw Santa Anna as a forceful, larger-than-life character during a time when few Mexican officials showed strong leadership abilities.

Unfortunately for Mexico, every one of Santa Anna's terms in office ended in some kind of political or military failure, usually bringing bloodshed and humiliation to the Mexican people. For instance, he captured the Alamo, but then went down to defeat at San Jacinto, where he was captured by Texans. Later, he lost a leg fighting the French and became a hero, only to be exiled to Cuba for incompetence shortly afterward. Though he was, at times, extremely popular, he was a remarkably poor leader.

Historians contend Gen. Antonio Lopez de Santa Anna was arrogant and self-centered. Santa Anna was personally affronted when Texas tried to challenge Mexican rule.

"In truth," commented historian Donald Chidsey, "he was not much of a general, and won his battles only when the forces under him enormously outnumbered those of the enemy." Arrogant and self-centered, Santa Anna enjoyed being called "most serene highness" and "the Napoleon of the West." Because of this arrogance and his notorious inability to plan ahead, he needlessly wasted thousands of Mexican lives in battle after battle.

Santa Anna did have an amazing ability, however, to gain the trust and allegiance of his people. He had a magnetic personality that commanded attention and respect, and his notorious outbursts of temper struck fear into the hearts of his soldiers. Yet he could also be dignified and gracious, and he always won the attention of the ladies at social gatherings. The wife of an American diplomat described him as "a gentlemanly, good-looking, quietly-dressed, rather melancholy person." A unique combination of ruthless tyrant and well-bred gentleman, "Santa Anna *was* Mexico in its early days as a republic," according to Chidsey.

In this nineteenth-century illustration, captured General Santa Anna (bowing) presents himself to an injured Sam Houston after the battle of San Jacinto.

Mexican camp. Houston, leading the charge, was heard to yell, "Hold your fire! God damn it, hold your fire!" He wanted his men to get close enough so that the first volley would devastate the enemy defenses. And it did. Taken totally by surprise, most of the Mexican sentries were killed in the first blast of Texan gunfire. The survivors immediately ran for their lives. Screaming "Remember the Alamo!" and "Remember Goliad!" the Texans swarmed into the Mexican camp. Before the startled Mexican troops could muster a defense, the Texans attacked them with handguns and bowie knives. The bloody hand-to-hand fighting did not last long. Realizing they had no chance, most of the Mexicans quickly surrendered.

Spare the Survivors

The battle of San Jacinto lasted less than twenty minutes. In that time, the Texans killed more than 700 Mexicans and captured another 730, including Santa Anna himself. Texan casualties were only nine killed and thirty wounded. Fearing they would suffer the same fate as the men at Goliad, many of the Mexican prisoners fell to their knees and murmured, "Me no Alamo!" over and over. Houston knew that this was a lie. But he refused to murder unarmed prisoners as he knew Santa Anna had. Houston ordered that the survivors be spared.

Hearing of Houston's victory, Texans and Americans alike were jubilant. They assumed that the trouble was finally over. After all, Texas had declared itself independent, and the Texans had defeated Santa Anna's army in a fair fight. Nearly twenty-five hundred Mexican troops had died in Texas. Most Texans believed that the Mexican government would not waste more of its soldiers' lives on the faraway border province. It seemed that there was nothing left now to stop a free Texas from enjoying peace and prosperity. But the situation was not so simple. For one thing, the Mexican government never recognized the existence of the Lone Star Republic. The Mexicans believed that the Texans had won merely a temporary victory and that Texas was still a part of Mexico. According to the Mexicans, the Texans were rebels and criminals who had seized Mexican territory. Mexican leaders vowed that, sooner or later, they would drive out the yanquis and regain control of Texas. The trouble was far from over. It was just beginning.

CHAPTER THREE

To Annex or Not to Annex? Mexico Issues a Warning

The dust of the San Jacinto battlefield had barely settled when many Texans began to clamor for American statehood. They cited two major reasons for wanting to become part of the United States. First, they believed that Texas could not long remain independent without the help of the United States. They pointed out that the Mexicans vastly outnumbered the Texans. By the end of 1836, the Texan population was approximately fifty thousand, while the population of Mexico was more than eight million. Mexico could obviously raise much larger armies and produce more weapons. Many of those who supported annexation, or the incorporation of Texas into the United States, believed that the victory at San Jacinto had been a lucky break. They feared that Mexico would send more and larger armies to fight the Texans and that sooner or later, the enemy's superior numbers would prevail.

Most of the Texans who favored statehood also cited the fact that a majority of the Texans were former Americans who were still linked to the United States by background, religion, and language. Texans realized that statehood would bring not only protection against Mexico but also the benefits of U.S. citizenship.

Many citizens in the United States were also in favor of annexing Texas. Some of these people were expansionists, or those who believed that the United States should acquire as much new territory as possible to accommodate its ever-growing population. They knew that making Texas a state might mean war with Mexico. But they actually welcomed such a conflict. They believed that a victorious United States would be in a position to seize even more Mexican territory.

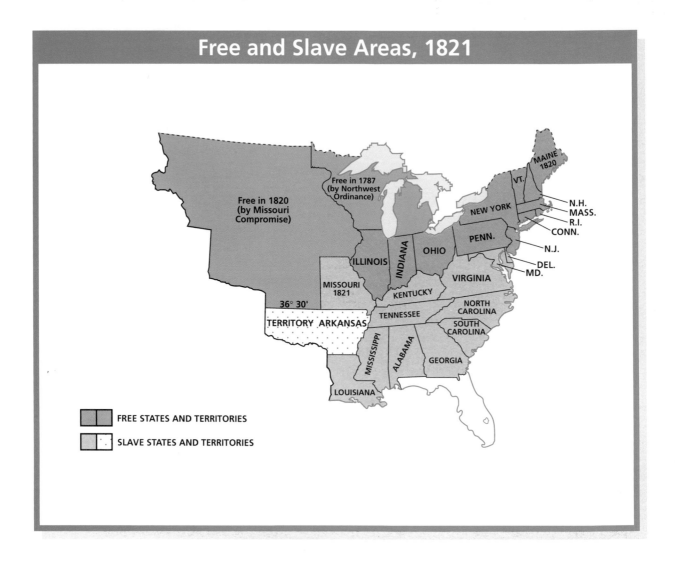

Free and Slave Areas, 1821

Free in 1820
(by Missouri
Compromise)

Free in 1787
(by Northwest
Ordinance)

MAINE
1820

VT.

NEW YORK

N.H.
MASS.
R.I.
CONN.

ILLINOIS

INDIANA

OHIO

PENN.

N.J.

DEL.
MD.

MISSOURI
1821

KENTUCKY

VIRGINIA

36° 30'

TERRITORY ARKANSAS

TENNESSEE

NORTH
CAROLINA

SOUTH
CAROLINA

MISSISSIPPI

ALABAMA

GEORGIA

LOUISIANA

FREE STATES AND TERRITORIES

SLAVE STATES AND TERRITORIES

A New Slave State

Other annexationists were southern politicians and businessmen
who saw Texas statehood as a way to spread the institution of
slavery. Many of the Texans already owned slaves, and annexing
Texas would add a new slave state to the union. In fact, there
were rumors that Texas, a huge territory, might be admitted as
two or three separate slave states. Each would have the standard
two votes in the Senate, thus increasing the power of slavehold-
ing states in the legislature. The slave states already held almost
as much power as the free states.

Fearing that the admission of Texas would give southern
states control of the Congress, most Northerners opposed annexation. Many in the North saw slavery as an evil institution that
should be abolished. Former president John Quincy Adams, then
a member of the House of Representatives, led the fight against
annexation. He and twelve colleagues published a pamphlet

The Issue of Slavery

All through the early decades of the nineteenth century, the differences between the American North and South grew more distinct. The northern states became increasingly industrialized, eliminating the need for slave labor. As slavery became less necessary in the North, Northerners began to look at this institution differently. They began to see that it was morally wrong for one person to own another. Abolitionists, those who wanted to see slavery abolished, gradually grew in number and power in the North.

By contrast, the economy of the southern states continued to be based on agriculture. Landowners continued to rely heavily on slave labor to work the fields. Most Southerners resisted change and sought to keep their society and culture, including slavery, intact. There were a few abolitionists in the South, but they were looked upon as troublemakers.

By the 1830s, Congress was sharply divided between southern slave states and northern free states. The two groups constantly struggled for power. In addition to the problem of slavery, economic issues divided the two groups. For example, every time northern legislators proposed new taxes to benefit northern industries, southern lawmakers voted against the measure.

Texas became a burning issue between the North and the South because most Texans were former Southerners who owned slaves. Southerners favored annexing Texas, hoping to add another slave state to the union and increase their strength in Congress. Worried about the growth of "slave power," most Northerners opposed granting Texas statehood. In the 1840s, the annexation debate became so heated that many Americans, including former president John Quincy Adams, feared the union might crumble. This possibility loomed over the country during the next decade as the gulf between North and South continued to widen until a bitter civil war erupted.

Southerners were dependent on slavery and wanted Texas annexed to the U.S. as a pro-slavery state. Northerners opposed slavery and did not want Texas annexed.

In this nineteenth-century painting, Texan slaves transport cotton to market. Slavery's expansion from the South to Texas nearly split the union.

warning of "the undue ascendancy of the slave-holding power." Adams called annexing Texas a "nefarious [evil] project" that could bring about a dangerous division between the North and South and even a breakup of the country.

Some Americans were opposed to annexation because they thought the Texans were troublemakers and unworthy of citizenship. They believed that the Texans had caused the fight with Mexico by stubbornly refusing to obey Mexican laws. Those who felt this way formed a group called the Anti-Tex*ass* Legion, purposely misspelling *Texas* to insult their opponents. One of the Legion's leaders said that annexing Texas would cause "the introduction into the union of an unprincipled population of adventurers."

The outgoing president, Andrew Jackson, favored annexation, and the expansionists pushed him to fight for Texan statehood. But he feared that such a move so soon after the Texan victories over Mexico would hurt his country's image. One writer described his dilemma: "Prompt annexation…would make it look to Mexico—and indeed to the whole world—that the United States really had been behind those bands of armed men who infiltrated the frontier, and that the whole thing was, as Mexico had always claimed, a gigantic swindle. So, Jackson held his hand."

These pro- and anti-annexation arguments came to be a major theme in the presidential election of 1840. Jackson's successor, Martin Van Buren, ran against Gen. William Henry Harrison, hero of the Indian battle of Tippecanoe. Like Jackson, Van Buren was an annexationist. Also like Jackson, he had managed to avoid the issue during his years in the White House from 1836 to 1840.

But rumor had it that if reelected, Van Buren would push for Texan statehood. His opponents, the leaders of the Whig party who supported Harrison, had a problem. They believed that Harrison, who was against annexation, had a chance to carry the northern states. But he would surely lose the southern states, which demanded that Texas be annexed. To get the needed southern votes, the Whigs chose John Tyler, a Southerner and avowed annexationist, as Harrison's running mate. The Whigs reasoned that since the vice president customarily exercised no real power, Tyler's views on Texas would have little influence once he was in office.

But the Whigs' plan soon backfired. Harrison and Tyler won the election. Only one month after taking office, however, on April 4, 1841, Harrison died of pneumonia. To the dismay of the Whigs and others opposed to annexation, John Tyler, a staunch advocate for Texas statehood, was now president.

Narrow Defeats

With Tyler in the White House, Mexican leaders feared that the Americans might make bold moves to acquire Texas. The Mexican government repeatedly warned that Texas was still Mexican territory and any move to annex it would be considered an act of

John Quincy Adams (left) opposed the annexation of Texas. Andrew Jackson (center) and Martin Van Buren (above) supported it.

President John Tyler (left) wanted Texas to be part of the United States. Lone Star Republic president Mirabeau B. Lamar (right) wanted Texas to remain independent and to expand westward.

war. Tyler ignored these warnings, trying on several occasions to push annexation through the legislature. Each time, northern congressmen, fearing that annexing Texas would strengthen the South, narrowly defeated the measure.

In the meantime, some anti-annexation ideas gained support in Texas itself. Sam Houston, who served as the first officially elected president of the Lone Star Republic, was succeeded by Mirabeau B. Lamar, a former cavalry officer. Lamar firmly believed that Texas should not become part of the United States. Instead, he said, the Lone Star Republic should remain an independent country, stand up to Mexico, and boldly expand westward. He suggested that Mexico's outlying provinces of New Mexico and California might be persuaded to join Texas and create a Texan "empire" that would stretch to the Pacific Ocean.

Join the Texans

In 1841, Lamar sent twenty-two wagons filled with trade goods toward Sante Fe, the capital of the New Mexico province. The wagon train was guarded by 265 Texan infantrymen. Lamar's aim was to open up a trade route between New Mexico and Texas because the two states had little contact with each other at the time. He also hoped to convince the people of Sante Fe, many of whom were former Americans, to break away from Mexico and join the Texans.

Sam Houston, Texan Patriot

The leader of the Texan movement for independence, Sam Houston (1793–1863) played a central role in Texas politics for nearly thirty years. A former soldier, lawyer, congressman, and governor of Tennessee, Houston was a tall, imposing frontiersman. He often dressed in buckskins or Indian attire and was known for his honesty, fairness, and diligence. He had a fiery temper and fought many duels yet also proved to be a skilled diplomat and negotiator. As a military leader, Houston enjoyed singing and telling tall tales with his men, whom he fought alongside in battle.

In 1832, President Jackson sent Houston to Texas to negotiate treaties with the local Indians. Taking a liking to the area, Houston settled there permanently and became active in Texas politics. In November 1835, when fighting broke out between the Texans and Mexicans, he took charge of the tiny Texan army. On April 21, 1836, he led that army to a decisive victory over the Mexicans at San Jacinto.

Houston's military successes, integrity, and flamboyant personality endeared him to the people of Texas. In the years that followed, they repeatedly called upon him to lead them. He served as president of the Lone Star Republic twice (1836–1838 and 1841–1844), as U.S. senator from the state of Texas (1845–1859), and as governor of the state (1859–1861).

Sam Houston (above) played a pivotal role in the history of Texas. He first led Texans to independence in 1836 and later served as president, senator, and governor of Texas. A map of Texas (left), circa 1845, shows the southern boundary defined by the Rio Grande.

The Mexicans, still insisting that Texas was a part of Mexico, saw Lamar's move as an act of treason and rebellion. A large force of Mexican troops hurried to Sante Fe in advance of the wagon train and captured the Texans when they arrived. The Mexicans marched the Texan prisoners nearly two thousand miles and locked them in the forbidding Perote fortress near Mexico City. Several Texans died from exhaustion or exposure during the trip, and the affair caused angry reactions in both Texas and the United States. Tyler and other annexationists pointed to the incident as proof that the United States must grant Texas statehood in order to protect it from the "cruel" and "bloodthirsty" Mexicans.

In the Lone Star Republic's 1841 election, Sam Houston defeated Mirabeau Lamar and became president once again. Public outrage pressured Houston to retaliate against the Mexicans for imprisoning the members of the Sante Fe expedition. Some Texan patriots demanded a full-scale war against Mexico. Houston wisely vetoed this idea. But in October 1842, he decided to dispatch 750 troops across the Rio Grande as a show of force. He reasoned that this would send a warning to the Mexicans that the Texans would not tolerate further interference in their affairs. He hoped the troops would show Mexico that Texans were able and willing to retaliate if necessary. But what was meant to be a "peaceful" show of force quickly turned into a nasty struggle.

On the way home, 360 of the Texan troops refused to leave. While the rest of the Texans recrossed the Rio Grande, the deserters stayed and, against Houston's orders, attacked the Mexican town of Mier. Within hours, a large force of Mexican troops surrounded them. The two groups fought hard for three days, and finally, the Texans surrendered. The Mexicans promptly shot forty of them and marched the rest to the Perote fortress.

Anti-Mexican Sentiments

When news of the latest Texan defeat was reported in the United States, anti-Mexican sentiments reached a fever pitch. Conservative American politicians demanded that the United States declare war on Mexico. In response, Señor Bocanegra, the Mexican minister of foreign affairs, issued a blunt and strongly worded statement to the Americans. He accused the U.S. government of purposely inciting the Texans to rebel. He warned that Mexico was tired of these relentless attacks by armed pirates and would, if further provoked, take action. Bocanegra insisted that the United States stay out of Mexican affairs and, above all, leave Texas alone. The Mexican leaders felt justified in delivering their harsh and clearly threatening ultimatum. Would the Americans heed the warning?

CHAPTER FOUR

Destiny of the "Superior Race"– War Is Declared

As the U.S. presidential election of 1844 neared, tensions rose in Mexico City. The Mexican leaders nervously watched as statehood for Texas once again became a central campaign issue. To the Mexicans, the election seemed like a dangerous repeat of the one in 1840. During the intervening four years, the Mexicans had warned the United States repeatedly that annexing Texas would mean war. They realized that if an annexationist won the 1844 election and Texas joined the union, Mexico would have to declare war on the United States.

Many Mexicans wanted to avoid such a conflict because they believed they had little chance of winning a war with the United States. Leading the antiwar faction was the new Mexican president, Jose Joaquin Herrera. He realized that his country was ill-prepared to wage a full-scale war. In the first place, the morale of the Mexican troops was at an all-time low because there was not enough money in the treasury to pay them.

Herrera also considered the U.S. population advantage. Although the United States had a much smaller standing army than Mexico, it had more than twice as many people and could easily raise the necessary troops.

Firepower was another important factor. The United States was a heavily industrialized country with dozens of cannon factories. By contrast, Mexico had almost no heavy industry and few cannon factories. In addition, the United States had a powerful navy, while Mexico had no navy at all. Herrera believed that a war between the two countries would be like the legendary encounter between David and Goliath, only this time David would have no sling.

President James K. Polk wanted to increase the size of the United States.

In November 1844, the Mexicans anxiously waited for news of the U.S. election results. They hoped that the Whig party candidate, Henry Clay, would win because Clay openly opposed both annexation and war. The nominee of the Democratic party, James K. Polk, was a staunch expansionist who favored annexing Texas.

A Difficult Position

When Polk won the election, Herrera and his colleagues found themselves in a difficult position. They had to uphold the honor of their country and stop the Americans from taking Texas. But they needed to do it without getting involved in a potentially disastrous war. There was obviously little chance of changing Polk's mind about annexation, so negotiation would be difficult. There seemed to be no choice but for Mexico to continue its hard-line stance and hope it would deter the Americans from grabbing Texas. After the election, the Mexicans once more warned the United States that annexation would be construed as an act of war.

But the Americans were not scared. They knew they would have clear advantage over Mexico if war broke out and ignored the Mexican warnings. Through the combined efforts of outgoing President Tyler and incoming President Polk, Congress passed the proposal for Texas annexation on March 1, 1845. Texas was now officially a part of the United States. This, at least, was the American position. The Mexicans had a completely different viewpoint. According to the Mexican ambassador in Washington, D.C., the United States had illegally taken control of Mexican territory. He immediately requested his passport and returned to Mexico City, breaking off diplomatic relations with the United States. Furious and insulted, Herrera and his advisers waited for Polk to make the next move.

The New Boundary

Polk acted quickly. On November 10, 1845, he sent his special negotiator, John Slidell, to Mexico. Slidell's orders were to offer the Mexicans five million dollars for New Mexico and twenty-five million dollars for California. The United States would pay these amounts provided that Mexico recognize the Rio Grande as the new boundary between the two countries. Polk hoped to nearly double the size of the United States in one bold stroke. He especially wanted California, whose ports would give the country access to the Pacific Ocean and its valuable trade routes with the Orient. Polk felt he must move fast, before either Great Britain, Russia, or France, all of which considered California to be valuable territory, made a deal with the Mexicans.

Differing Military Attitudes

I n 1845, the American military tradition was only seventy years old, having begun during the Revolutionary War. The first American soldiers were the minutemen, soldier-farmers who grabbed their muskets on a moment's notice, fought a battle, then returned home to harvest their crops. By the time of the Mexican War, attitudes in the United States toward the military had not changed much. The soldiers were mostly volunteers, many of whom did not take military service seriously. Discipline was lax, desertions were common, and formal training was minimal. To many Americans, the country's small standing army seemed almost useless. By the 1840s, Congress considered closing down the West Point National Military Academy as an unnecessary expense.

In sharp contrast, Mexico boasted a proud military tradition that stretched back more than three hundred years. As a longtime Spanish colony, the country inherited the European, or "continental," military system. The Mexican government maintained a large standing army as a matter of course. Serving in the army was considered an honor, and long-term professional careers were encouraged. Discipline was strict, and those who broke the rules were severely punished, so there were usually few deserters.

The importance and prestige of the military in Mexican life was reflected in the attitudes of the young. Many Mexican boys dreamed of attending the National Military Academy, housed in the former palace of the Spanish viceroys on Chapultepec Hill in Mexico City. By the 1840s, public pride in the country's military traditions had made the academy one of the most well-maintained and respected institutions in Mexico.

During the Mexican-American War, American troops retained the loosely knit attitude of the Revolutionary War's minutemen (left). Mexican troops were more formal in attire (above) and attitude.

On hearing that Slidell had arrived in Mexico, Herrera called a meeting of the Mexican cabinet. Some members called the Slidell mission an insult. First, the Americans had stolen Texas. Now they wanted to further reduce Mexico's size and power by robbing the country of its Pacific ports. They demanded an immediate declaration of war against the "uncivilized yanquis." Herrera urged caution. Perhaps they could negotiate with Slidell and avoid a costly war. But the others convinced Herrera that a meeting with Slidell would be an admission that the Texas crisis was over, that Mexico had lost Texas. So Herrera refused to meet with Slidell.

When Slidell sent word to Washington that he had been slighted by the Mexicans, Polk reacted angrily. Believing the incident to be an insult to the United States, Polk began searching for some excuse to force the Mexicans into war. He felt sure that most Americans would eagerly back such an enterprise.

Polk knew that expansionism and war with Mexico were controversial issues. Many Americans strongly opposed both. But

Americans were excited about news of the possibility of war with Mexico. Some Americans opposed war. Others wanted the nation to expand.

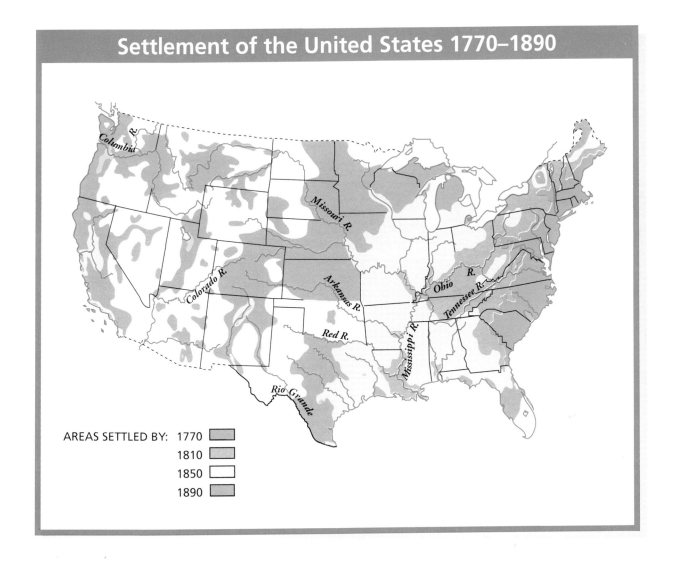

Settlement of the United States 1770–1890

AREAS SETTLED BY: 1770
1810
1850
1890

many others were eager to see the country expand, even if it meant war. Polk seemed confident that a majority of Americans agreed with him that the country should expand "from sea to shining sea."

Many newspapers of the day came out in favor of the expansionist viewpoint. For example, in 1845, the *Washington Union,* a newspaper that backed Polk and other Democrats, insisted that westward expansion into Mexican lands was inevitable. An editorial in the paper asked:

> For who can arrest the torrent that will pour onward to the West? The road to California will be open to us. Who will stay [stop] the march of our western people?

Openly approving of the idea of war, the *Union* added:

> A corps of properly organized volunteers...would invade, overrun, and occupy Mexico. They would enable us not only to take California, but to keep it.

Manifest Destiny

Between 1820 and 1845, the U.S. population more than doubled to twenty million. As the number of Americans increased, more and more people headed westward, and the idea of an ever-expanding United States became increasingly popular. Millions of acres of priceless, undeveloped territory stretched before the American people. Many came to believe that this good fortune was evidence that God intended white Americans to rule from the Atlantic to the Pacific. In 1845, John O'Sullivan, editor of the popular *Democratic Review,* summed up the expansionist doctrine, saying that it was "Our manifest destiny to overspread the continent allotted by Providence [God's will] for the free development of our expanding millions." American settlers later used the idea of manifest destiny to justify their dishonest, often cruel and racist treatment of the Indians and Mexicans who already occupied western lands. For example, the Americans repeatedly broke treaties with the Indians, who they looked upon as dumb savages. From whites' twisted point of view, it seemed unthinkable that God could have created so many abundant lands for the use of mere savages.

Shortly after these remarks appeared, one newspaper editor suggested that God had created the vast lands of the American frontier specifically for the use of the people of the United States. It was the God-given right and ultimate fate of Americans to seize control of the entire North American continent. He called this fate "manifest destiny," and the term immediately became popular.

White Superiority

Those who embraced manifest destiny assumed that since God intended the United States to control the continent, there must be something special about Americans. This idea was partially racist—it reinforced the belief of a majority of people in the United States that white, Protestant Americans were superior to most other peoples. It provided a convenient justification for pushing aside the millions of Mexicans and Indians who stood in the way of white expansion. These people, many Americans believed, were inferior races who must give way to their white masters. Southern slave owners were not the only ones who held this view. Many Northerners also subscribed to it.

Major newspapers as well as respected politicians and clergymen openly advocated expansionism for racist reasons. The influential *American Review* said that Mexico should bow before "a superior population, insensibly oozing into her territories, changing her customs, and out-living, out-trading, exterminating her weaker blood."

The Rev. Theodore Parker of Boston called the Mexicans "a wretched people; wretched in their origin, history and character." He referred to American expansion as the "steady advance of a superior race, with superior ideas and a better civilization." And an Ohio congressman described Mexicans as an inferior people who "embrace all shades of color...a sad compound of Spanish, English, Indian and negro bloods...and resulting, it is said, in the production of a slothful, ignorant race of beings." Although many Americans rejected these views as racist and unfair, a majority did accept them.

Provoked into Fighting

President Polk decided to take advantage of manifest destiny's growing popularity. He strongly believed that a war with Mexico would win the United States valuable Mexican territories, especially California and its Pacific ports. Expecting that a majority of Americans would support him, Polk decided to actually provoke the Mexicans into fighting.

Late in 1845, Polk ordered Gen. Zachary Taylor to take four thousand men, more than half the American army at that time, to

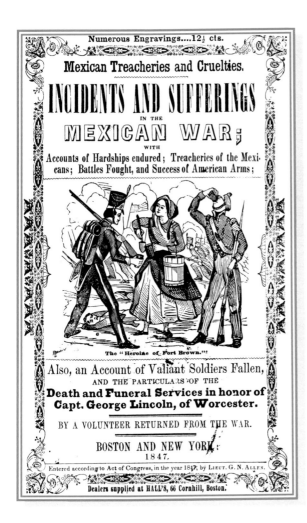

Numerous Engravings....12½ cts.

Mexican Treacheries and Cruelties.

INCIDENTS AND SUFFERINGS

IN THE

MEXICAN WAR;

WITH

Accounts of Hardships endured; Treacheries of the Mexicans; Battles Fought, and Success of American Arms;

The "Heroine of Fort Brown."

Also, an Account of Valiant Soldiers Fallen,

AND THE PARTICULARS OF THE

Death and Funeral Services in honor of Capt. George Lincoln, of Worcester.

BY A VOLUNTEER RETURNED FROM THE WAR.

BOSTON AND NEW YORK:
1847.

Entered according to Act of Congress, in the year 1847, by LIEUT. G. N. ALLEN.

Dealers supplied at HALL'S, 66 Cornhill, Boston.

This book (left) described the "Mexican Treacheries and Cruelties" of the war. (Below) Mexican soldiers strip dead American soldiers on a battlefield, circa 1845.

Texas. The soldiers camped at Corpus Christi, near the Nueces River, about two hundred miles north of the Rio Grande.

The Mexicans officially recognized the Nueces as the southern Texas border, while the Americans considered the Rio Grande to mark the border. Since the Americans had already annexed Texas, they considered all the lands north of the Rio Grande to be American soil. The Mexicans, on the other hand, contended that all of Texas was still part of Mexico. They were outraged that American troops had entered Texas, but they still wanted to avoid a fight if they could. They decided not to react unless the yanquis crossed the Nueces.

Polk grew frustrated by the Mexicans' restraint. In January 1846, he commanded Taylor to cross the Nueces. One of Taylor's men, Col. Ethan Allen Hitchcock, was disturbed about the warlike tactics of his superiors. He recorded in his diary:

He [Taylor] is immediately to proceed with his whole command to the extreme western border of Texas and take up a position on the banks of…the Rio Grande, and he is to expel

Zachary Taylor, "Old Rough and Ready"

"Anything but the very model of a modern major general" is the way one writer described Zachary Taylor (1784–1850). Taylor, a small, clumsy man with a weather-beaten face, liked to dress in sloppy, backwoods clothes and almost always wore a dirty, wrinkled handkerchief around his neck. Called "Old Zack" and "Old Rough and Ready" by his men, Taylor rode his horse, Old Whitey, sidesaddle, as a woman would.

Despite his odd appearance and habits, Taylor was an experienced soldier and able leader. His first military commission came in 1808 from President Thomas Jefferson. Later, Taylor served in the War of 1812 and in the Seminole Indian War of 1835. His exploits in the Mexican War made him a national hero, and the Whig party decided to take advantage of his popularity. Taylor ran as the Whig presidential candidate in 1848, and he won. Unfortunately, he never had a chance to prove his political worth, for he died of food poisoning a little more than a year after assuming office.

Zachary Taylor was known as "Old Zack" or "Old Rough and Ready." He served in the War of 1812, the Seminole Indian War of 1835, and in the Mexican-American War.

American troops fire upon Matamoros in this nineteenth-century lithograph.

any armed force of Mexicans who may cross the river…. Violence leads to violence, and if this movement of ours does not lead to others and to bloodshed, I am much mistaken.

Taylor and his troops camped directly across the river from the town of Matamoros. The Mexican general, Pedro de Ampudia, arrived in the town a few days later with two thousand troops. Ampudia ordered Taylor to return to the Nueces within twenty-four hours or the Mexicans would be forced to take action. Taylor arrogantly responded by building a fort. "He seems to have lost all respect for Mexican rights and is willing to be an instrument of Mr. Polk for pushing our boundary as far west as possible," wrote Colonel Hitchcock.

A few days later, the Mexicans made good on their threat to take action. Gen. Mariano Arista arrived with reinforcements and took charge of the Matamoros garrison. Seeing that the Americans had not retreated, Arista ordered sixteen hundred cavalry to cross the river and take up positions a few miles from the American fort. He hoped this show of force would persuade Taylor to retreat.

Shedding American Blood

Arista did not realize that this was the move the American general had been waiting for. Taylor, preparing for battle, dispatched a sixty-three-man patrol to scout the enemy's location and strength.

On April 26, 1846, the Americans stopped to rest at a ranch house. There, the Mexicans promptly surrounded them, and shots rang out. It remains uncertain who fired first. The exchange of gunfire lasted only a few minutes but ended with eleven Americans dead and most of the others wounded or captured. Only four managed to escape and reach the American camp. Taylor quickly sent a message to Polk. He told the president that the Mexicans had shed American blood on American soil, a reference to the recent annexation of the area. "Hostilities may now be considered as commenced," Taylor added.

President Polk received Taylor's letter on May 10. By that time, most of the country had heard about the events on the Nueces River. As Polk began drafting a declaration of war, a number of prominent Americans immediately expressed their displeasure with the events on the Rio Grande. They were part of the country's minority against expansionism, manifest destiny, and the U.S. annexation of Texas. Congressmen John Quincy Adams and Joshua Giddings called the actions of Polk and Taylor immoral. Their feelings and those of other angry Americans were reflected by an entry in Colonel Hitchcock's diary:

> I have said from the first that the United States are the aggressors.... We have not one particle of right to be here.... It looks as if the government sent a small force on purpose to bring on a war, so as to have a pretext for taking California and as much of this country as it chooses.... My heart is not in this business...but, as a military man, I am bound to execute orders.

Polk was undeterred by such sentiments. He finished his war declaration on May 11, 1846, and sent it to Congress. His words were dramatic and blunt:

> After reiterated [repeated] menaces, Mexico has passed the boundary of the United States, has invaded our territory and shed American blood upon the American soil.... As war exists, notwithstanding all our efforts to avoid it, exists by the act of Mexico herself, we are called upon by every consideration of duty and patriotism to vindicate with decision the honor, the rights, and the interests of our country.

Congress quickly reacted to Polk's declaration. The House of Representatives passed the measure that same afternoon by a vote of 173 to 14. The Senate passed it the next day, and on May 13 the president signed it. It was now official. The United States of America and the Republic of Mexico were joined in a death struggle for control of the continent.

CHAPTER FIVE

"A Soldier's Life Is Very Disgusting"—The United States Invades Mexico

Reactions in the United States to Polk's declaration of war were sharply divided. Not surprisingly, the expansionists were overjoyed. Their mood was captured by the poet Walt Whitman, who wrote in the *Brooklyn Eagle*, "Yes: Mexico must be thoroughly chastised [punished]!… Let our arms now be carried with a spirit which shall teach the world that, while we are not forward for a quarrel, America knows how to crush, as well as how to expand!" And the *Congressional Globe* editorialized, "We must march from Texas straight to the Pacific Ocean…. It is the destiny of the white race." Pro-war rallies and demonstrations occurred in New York, Baltimore, Philadelphia, and other cities, and thousands of men hurried to enlist in the army.

The antiwar voices, though few in number, were loud and expressive. Congressman Joshua Giddings led a small group of war dissenters in Washington, D.C. He called the fight with Mexico "an aggressive, unholy, and unjust war." He voted against supplying soldiers and weapons for the war, saying:

> In the murder of Mexicans upon their own soil, or in robbing them of their country, I can take no part either now or hereafter. The guilt of these crimes must rest on others—I will not participate in them.

Others agreed with Giddings, including a young congressman from Illinois named Abraham Lincoln. Though his views on the war were unpopular with most Americans, many respected him for his courage in standing up to the president. He repeatedly challenged Polk to show the specific spot where the Mexicans

As an Illinois congressman, Abraham Lincoln opposed the war with Mexico.

A Mexican soldier on horseback lances a Texan in this woodcut illustration.

Henry David Thoreau protested the Mexican-American War by refusing to pay his taxes. He was promptly jailed.

had "shed American blood on American soil." These challenges became known as Lincoln's "spot resolutions." The president consistently refused to answer Lincoln, who later said the war was "unnecessarily and unconstitutionally commenced" by Polk. Lincoln added:

> The marching an army into the midst of a peaceful Mexican settlement, frightening the inhabitants away, leaving their growing crops and other property to destruction, to you may appear a perfectly amiable, peaceful, unprovoking procedure; but it does not appear so to us.

A few Americans were willing to go to prison to protest the war. In Concord, Massachusetts, the writer Henry David Thoreau denounced the conflict and demonstrated against it by refusing to pay his taxes. The local authorities promptly threw him in jail. They released him when his friends paid his taxes against his wishes. Polk, confident that such protests did not represent the views of a majority of Americans, proceeded with military preparations.

A Battle of Personalities

It was clear to many people that the war would become, at least in part, a battle among four strong personalities. There was Polk himself, who had a reputation for being both unsociable and stubborn. He was also known for sitting quietly while his opponents spoke their minds. Some said this made him a good listener. Others said this was his way of searching for signs of weakness in his adversaries. Polk was deeply patriotic and had an almost fanatic desire to see the United States stretch its boundaries westward. He predicted that the country's superior industrial strength, especially the artillery factories in the North, would assure an easy victory over Mexico.

On the Mexican side, there was the arrogant, flamboyant Santa Anna, who had managed once more to win the support of his people. Proclaiming himself the "savior of Mexico," he accepted command of the army and promised to repel the "yanqui devils." He assured his colleagues that Mexico would not have to fight the entire United States. New England, New York, and Pennsylvania, he predicted, would secede from the union when the fighting began. The Mexicans would have to contend only with the southern and western states, which had smaller populations and few cannon factories.

The other two major figures in the war were American generals Zachary Taylor and Winfield Scott. In appearance and personality, they were complete opposites. Taylor was a sloppily dressed frontier type who enjoyed socializing with his men. By contrast, Scott was a formal, strictly disciplined soldier who

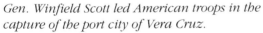

Gen. Winfield Scott led American troops in the capture of the port city of Vera Cruz.

These lithographs depict the battle of Palo Alto, fought by twenty-five hundred American troops and twice as many Mexicans. Artillery has mortally wounded an American officer (above). American troops (left) suffered fewer casualties than the Mexicans.

believed in doing things by the book. In spite of their differences, they had two things in common. They thoroughly disliked one another, and each wanted to be president eventually. It appeared that Taylor and Scott would be fighting two battles, one against the Mexicans and one against each other for national recognition.

Taylor, with the advantage of already being in Texas, scored the first points. On May 8, 1846, he led a force of twenty-five hundred men against twice as many Mexicans under Gen. Arista at Palo Alto, just north of the Rio Grande. The two armies faced each other on a flat stretch of open prairie. There was a devastating artillery exchange, during which the American cannons inflicted heavy losses on the Mexicans. The Mexican cannons consistently fired too low, causing the cannonballs to bounce short of the American lines. In less than one hour, the prairie grass caught fire, and under cover of the smoke, both armies pulled back and regrouped.

Hand-to-Hand Combat

A day later, Taylor attacked the Mexicans at a dried-up riverbed known as Resaca de la Palma. The battle, fought mainly hand to hand, was an unusually bloody affair. A young American lieutenant named Ulysses S. Grant witnessed "a ball crash into ranks nearby, tear a musket from one soldier's grasp and rip off the man's head, then dissect the face" of a captain he knew. Artillery-man Samuel French saw a shell strike a man on horseback, then:

> rip off the pommel of the saddle, tear through the man's body, and burst out with a crimson gush on the other side. Pieces of bone or metal tore into the horse's hip, split the lip and tongue and knocked teeth out of a second horse and broke the jaw of a third.

As the Americans cut their way through the Mexican camp, General Arista fled from his tent and most of his surviving men followed him in retreat.

While the defeated Mexicans escaped across the Rio Grande, Taylor tallied up the spoils of his victory. The Americans had captured all the Mexican cannons and supplies, six hundred mules, and hundreds of muskets. In all, the Mexicans lost more

Before his presidency, Ulysses S. Grant (left) served as a lieutenant in the Mexican-American War. He fought in many battles, including Resaca de la Palma (below and below left). He witnessed the damage that war can cause.

The Mexican-American War 1846–1848

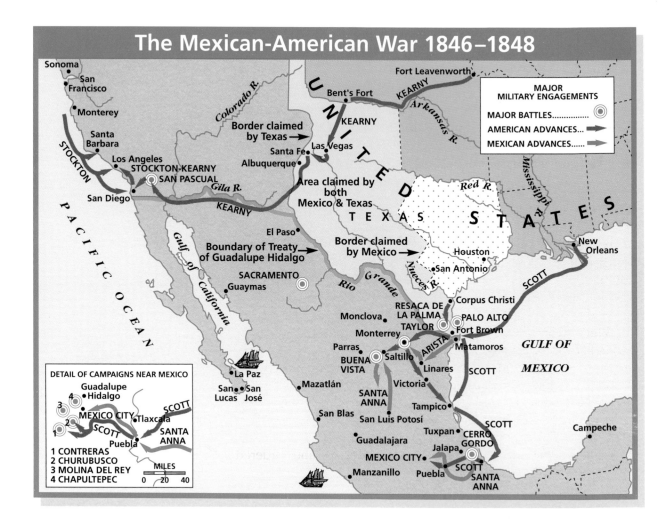

than eight hundred men, while the American dead numbered just over one hundred. This first official engagement of the war had been a triumph for Old Rough and Ready. His satisfaction at winning increased when he leapt from his horse and entered Arista's tent. There, to his delight, Taylor found a letter from the Mexican president ordering Arista to smash the American army and bring Zachary Taylor in chains to Mexico City.

Meanwhile, Gen. Stephen W. Kearny had raised a force of fifteen hundred frontiersmen near Fort Leavenworth on the Missouri River. Dubbing his command "the army of the West," Kearny marched his men one thousand miles in six weeks and arrived in Santa Fe on August 18, 1846. Hearing of the Americans' approach, the Mexican garrison under Governor Armijo fled, so Kearny encountered no resistance. He issued a statement announcing that all the inhabitants of New Mexico were hereby American citizens, then officially proclaimed himself governor. The Americans had taken control of thousands of square miles of territory containing some eighty thousand people without firing a shot.

In American Hands

Kearny quickly set his sights on achieving another important American goal—taking over the territory of California. He hired the famous frontiersman Kit Carson to guide him and three hundred men to Los Angeles. His prompt arrival turned out to be timely and strategically important. A small American military expedition, commanded by Commodore Robert F. Stockton and Capt. John C. Fremont, had recently landed in California. Mexican troops, however, quickly drove the expedition out of southern California. When Kearny arrived, he immediately joined forces with Stockton and Fremont. The Americans then counterattacked, driving the Mexicans out of Los Angeles and San Diego. By the end of 1846, California, the prize that Polk and the expansionists desired most, was in American hands. The United States was now in control of all the Mexican borderland from the Gulf of Mexico to the Pacific Ocean.

While Kearny took control of New Mexico, the disgraced General Arista faced a court-martial in Mexico City. His successor was Gen. Francisco Mejia, a well-spoken man known for wearing blue sunglasses. Mejia knew that Zachary Taylor was headed toward Monterrey, located about one hundred miles south of the Rio Grande. The city occupied a strategic position, just north of the central Mexican plateau, the region where most Mexicans lived. Mejia reinforced Arista's shattered forces and ordered seven thousand troops to defend Monterrey.

In this lithograph, troops led by Gen. Zachary Taylor march toward Monterrey.

American troops storm a Mexican fortress during the battle of Monterrey.

It was raining hard on September 21, 1846, when Taylor attacked Monterrey. The Americans surrounded the city and closed in. They were surprised when they encountered fierce resistance. Previously, they had easily defeated the Mexicans in battles on the open plains. This time was different. Defending the ten thousand civilians of Monterrey, the Mexican troops fought savagely and with great distinction.

For three days, as the rain continued, the battle raged both inside and outside the city. The fighting was chaotic. The soldiers clashed in mostly hand-to-hand combat, slashing with bayonets and clubbing each other with rifle butts. The Mexicans constantly held their ground, and the Americans had to take the city street by street, house by house. Losses on both sides were heavy.

The Mexicans Surrender

Realizing that the bloody battle might continue for several more days, the Americans finally tried a different strategy. They pointed their cannons at the local cathedral and threatened to blow it up. The threat worked. The devoutly religious Mexicans reluctantly surrendered. Many of the American troops then ran wild through the captured city, looting, burning houses, raping women, and killing whole families.

The slaughter in Monterrey was so terrible that it sent a wave of revulsion through the United States. An anonymous letter to the *Cambridge Chronicle* denounced the "'glorious' butcheries of women and children as were displayed in the capture of Monterrey." William Lloyd Garrison's newspaper, the *Liberator,* spoke of the war as one "of aggression, of invasion, of conquest, and rapine—marked by ruffianism…and other features of national depravity." Horace Greeley wrote in the *New York Tribune:*

> We can easily defeat the armies of Mexico, slaughter them by the thousands, and pursue them perhaps to their capital…but what then? Who believes that a score of victories over Mexico…will give us more liberty, a purer Morality…. Is not Life miserable enough, comes Death not soon enough, without resort to the hideous enginery of War?

Taylor himself admitted to "some shameful atrocities" by his men. But he pointed out that the soldiers were under great pressure. Most, he said, hated what they were doing, disliked the strict discipline of army life, and just wanted to go home. One Pennsylvania volunteer under Taylor's command remarked, "A

Fierce and bloody combat broke out as U.S. troops entered Monterrey's central plaza.

American soldiers in camp wash clothes (above) and prepare to cook freshly caught game (right).

soldier's life is very disgusting." Taylor agreed, but he did not think that this justified the murder of civilians, and he publicly condemned the crimes his men had committed. Yet Taylor did not take any disciplinary action to punish his troops. Polk, who apparently agreed with Taylor's assessment, said little about the incidents.

Undaunted by the storm of criticism, Taylor pushed on into the Mexican interior. On February 22, 1847, Taylor's army of some six thousand men reached the narrow pass of Buena Vista, about 150 miles southwest of Monterrey and some 500 miles north of Mexico City. There, they encountered a Mexican force of at least twenty thousand led by Santa Anna himself. The wily Mexican general had just declared himself dictator of Mexico once again, promising to crush the "barbarians" from the north.

Gen. Zachary Taylor (center, on horse) led six thousand men against twenty thousand Mexican troops at the battle of Buena Vista. After one day of bitter fighting, the Mexicans retreated south.

An All-Out Assault

The two armies camped for the night. The next morning, Santa Anna lined up his troops for an all-out assault on the Americans. He sent a message to Taylor, declaring that the Americans were outnumbered and should surrender. Taylor replied, "I regret that I must decline acceding to your request." Then, he had some of his men loudly play "Hail, Columbia," a patriotic American song.

A few minutes later, the Mexicans charged. But the Americans were in trenches, and the attackers found it difficult to maneuver in the narrow pass. The Americans beat back the charge. Soon, the Mexicans regrouped and charged again, but once more they had to retreat. This scenario was repeated over and over again until dusk. On each charge, there was bloody hand-to-hand fighting in the pass.

In the morning, the Americans were surprised to find that the Mexicans had gone. It was unclear why Santa Anna had retreated, although Taylor suggested that the Mexican losses had been heavy. The Mexicans had taken most of their dead with them when they left, yet more than five hundred Mexican corpses still lay in the field. Evidently, Santa Anna had headed south to defend the Mexican heartland. Taylor's losses were also heavy: 267 killed, 465 wounded, and 23 missing.

In the meantime, Taylor's political adversary, General Scott, raced his army of nearly fourteen thousand men toward the Mexican port of Vera Cruz. Located on the Gulf of Mexico only two hundred miles east of Mexico City, Vera Cruz was the strongest fortified city in the western hemisphere.

The Battle for Vera Cruz

On March 9, 1847, Gen. Winfield Scott landed fourteen thousand troops at Mocambo Bay, about three miles southeast of the highly fortified port city of Vera Cruz. There were approximately five thousand well-supplied Mexican soldiers within the city. Scott considered three alternatives. He could lay siege the city until the Mexicans ran out of supplies. But this would take months, and by that time yellow fever would strike the American army. Scott also considered attacking the huge city walls with massed infantry and scaling ladders. But this would cost perhaps thousands of American lives.

Scott decided on a third plan—an artillery bombardment from both land and sea. The barrage began on March 22 and continued for days. Col. Ethan Hitchcock, who had served in the north with General Taylor, wrote: "I shall never forget the horrible fire of our mortars… going with dreadful certainty… often in the centre of private dwellings—it was awful. I shudder to think of it."

Eventually, the Mexican commander, Gen. Juan de Landero, met with Scott to work out terms of surrender. The Mexicans feared that the "uncivilized" yanquis would try to destroy Catholic churches and nunneries. De Landero insisted that the people of Vera Cruz be allowed to worship unmolested. Scott agreed to this, and on March 28, the surrender took place. The defeated Mexican soldiers, many with tears in their eyes, handed over their weapons in an orderly manner. Grimly yet gallantly, they stood at attention as the Americans raised the Stars and Stripes above the city and a band played "Hail, Columbia."

Ten thousand American troops (top) land on the shores of Vera Cruz. Gen. Winfield Scott (left, on horse) leads his soldiers into battle against the Mexicans in the fortress at the city's port. While Scott attacks on land, American ships (above) fire upon the city from the harbor.

The Threat of Yellow Fever

Gen. Winfield Scott's fear that yellow fever might destroy his army in Mexico was well-founded. A disease that occurs in tropical regions, "yellow jack," as the illness is sometimes called, is spread by mosquitoes during the hot months of late spring and early summer. Symptoms on the first day after acquiring the disease are headache, sensitive skin, and drowsiness. Soon, the victim gets severe stomach pains and vomits black liquid. For this reason, the Mexicans called the disease *el vomito negro.* Within three days, the victim's skin turns green, and the eyes become yellow. Later, the gums and nose bleed. A person either dies on the fifth or sixth day or endures a slow, painful recovery.

Yellow fever is highly contagious, spreads quickly, and has been known to change the course of history. Between 1794 and 1803, for example, the disease killed more than forty thousand British and French troops sent to put down uprisings in the Caribbean island colony of Saint-Domingue. Decimated, or destroyed, by yellow fever, the Europeans fled the island, which then declared its independence and changed its name to Haiti.

A White Flag

Scott had good reason to hurry. If he arrived at the port after the middle of April, it would be yellow fever season and his men had no resistance to the disease. His army could be destroyed before a shot was fired. Driving his men hard, Scott reached Vera Cruz on March 9, 1847. On March 22, he began bombarding the city with heavy cannon fire. Six days later, the Mexican commander sent out a white flag indicating he would surrender.

The news of the fall of Vera Cruz shocked and terrified the people of Mexico City. All that stood between the captured port and the capital was the grand National Highway, which was largely undefended. The Mexicans began preparations for an assault by the Americans. There was only one hope now for the country. Somehow, Santa Anna had to ambush and annihilate the Americans before they reached the capital. As Scott marched inland from Vera Cruz, Santa Anna hastily maneuvered an army of more than twenty thousand to meet the American general and his troops.

CHAPTER SIX

At the Halls of Montezuma–Mexico Falls

As the American army marched out of Vera Cruz and headed for the Mexican capital, many of the men wondered what new surprises might lie ahead for them. Strangers in a strange land, they had already been astonished by much of what they had encountered. The huge size and excellent design of Vera Cruz's fortifications amazed them, as did the stately beauty of the city's streets and buildings. And there were the Mexicans themselves. Instead of the ignorant "greasers" portrayed by the popular stereotype, the Americans found a sophisticated, cultured, and courageous people.

After marching only a few miles north of Vera Cruz, the Americans discovered a new marvel—Mexico's National Highway. Stretching for hundreds of miles, the road connected Vera Cruz with Mexico City and other important towns. It was paved, graded, and equipped with gutters to carry off rainwater. Few American roads compared favorably to it. Somewhere along this highway, General Scott reasoned, Santa Anna would try to block the American advance.

With the Americans approaching on the National Highway, Mexico City was in an uproar. The government was in disarray as members of the cabinet and legislature frantically argued about how to stop the oncoming troops. People in the streets built barricades and tried to stockpile supplies. They were angry and bitter that the enemy had penetrated so far into Mexican territory. And they were afraid. Most Mexicans believed that the Americans were violent anti-Catholics who would destroy the city's churches, murder the priests, and rape the nuns. Many

VOLUNTEERS !

Men of the Granite State!

Men of Old Rockingham !! the strawberry-bed of patriotism, renowned for bravery and devotion to Country, rally at this call. Santa Anna, reeking with the generous confidence and magnanimity of your countrymen, is in arms, eager to plunge his traitor-dagger in their bosoms. To arms, then, and rush to the standard of the fearless and gallant **CUSHING**---put to the blush the dastardly meanness and rank toryism of Massachusetts. Let the half civilized Mexicans hear the crack of the unerring New Hampshire rifleman, and illustrate on the plains of San Luis Potosi, the fierce, determined, and undaunted bravery that has always characterized her sons.

Col. **THEODORE F. ROWE**, at No. 31 Daniel-street, is authorized and will enlist men this week for the Massachusetts Regiment of Volunteers. The compensation is **$10 per month---$30 in advance.** Congress will grant a handsome bounty in money and **ONE HUNDRED AND SIXTY ACRES OF LAND.**

Portsmouth, Feb. 2. 1847.

This wartime poster, printed in 1847, seeks to recruit young men of the northeastern states to join the battles in Mexico.

Mexicans vowed they would fight to the last citizen against the "barbaric and cruel" Americans. The people of the capital prayed that Santa Anna would accomplish a miracle and save the city.

An American Victory

As Scott had anticipated, Santa Anna chose to confront the troops along the highway. The Mexican general hoped either to decisively defeat the Americans or to keep them pinned down in the low, hot coastal region until the onset of yellow fever season. The disease would then cripple the enemy, assuring a Mexican victory.

Santa Anna set up his line of defense at Cerro Gordo, a tiny village about a dozen miles inland from Vera Cruz. The village was located on the banks of a deep, swiftly moving stream near a cluster of steep hills lining the highway. He heavily fortified the village, the road, and El Telegrapho, the highest hill in the area. He decided not to fortify some of the other hills since they were so steep and rough. He reasoned that the Americans would not be able to pull their artillery up and down these slopes and would choose instead to attack the village.

But Santa Anna had badly underestimated the abilities of the American military engineers who told General Scott that it was possible for an American force to scale the unfortified hills. This would allow them to attack the enemy from the rear and pin the Mexicans down on the banks of the stream. Scott quickly approved the plan.

Mexican soldiers, shown here in full battle dress, were confident that the onset of the yellow fever season would cripple U.S. troops.

On April 17, 1847, the engineers, led by young Capt. Robert E. Lee, went into action. They swiftly anchored posts in the hillsides, attaching complex arrangements of block and tackle to the posts. With incredible speed, they created a conveyer system to move cannons, men, and supplies up and down the nearly vertical cliffs. Lt. Ulysses Grant, who would later become Lee's Civil War adversary, watched in amazement. In his memoirs, Grant recorded:

> The walls were so steep that men could barely climb them. Animals could not.... The engineers, who had directed the opening, led the way and the troops followed. Artillery was let down the steep slopes by hand, the men engaged attaching a strong rope to the rear axle and letting the guns down, a piece at a time, while the men at the ropes kept their ground at the top, paying out gradually.... In a like manner the guns were drawn by hand up the opposite slopes.

These nineteenth-century lithographs depict the battle fought at Cerro Gordo, near Vera Cruz. Much of the fighting entailed hand-to-hand combat (top). Gen. Winfield Scott (left, on horseback) led his troops to victory.

The next day, the Americans attacked from several directions at once. Some approached the village, while others assaulted El Telegrapho. Only minutes later, the men and artillery that had scaled the cliffs created a flanking movement that caught the Mexicans by surprise. Scott's cannons now faced the Mexicans on three sides. Santa Anna realized that if he tried to fight, his men would be ripped apart by the American cannons. There would be no army left to defend Mexico City. He immediately ordered a retreat toward the capital. The order was unnecessary. Most of the Mexicans, seeing that they were hopelessly trapped, were already running for their lives. There were very few casualties in what could be better described as a skirmish than a battle. The Americans captured about three thousand Mexican troops. Scott disarmed and released them, under the condition that they stay out of the remainder of the fighting.

Soldiers from Mexican and American armies engage in fierce fighting at the battle of Cerro Gordo in this nineteenth-century lithograph. Mexican troops later retreated deeper into Mexico.

Enough of a Victory

While General Scott continued his march toward Mexico City, many antiwar meetings and rallies were held in U.S. cities. Critics of what some now called "Mr. Polk's war" asked why the Mexican capital had to be attacked. Had not the Americans already crushed the Mexican army? Did not the president already have enough of a victory to force his territorial demands?

General Santa Anna (top, on horse) flees the scene of the battle at Cerro Gordo. After beating the Mexicans there, General Scott (above) continued moving his troops south, toward Mexico City. Once there, Lt. Ulysses S. Grant (right) directed his men to hoist cannons to the top of a church, from which they fired upon the city.

Frederick Douglass, the writer and former slave, spoke of "the present disgraceful, cruel, and iniquitous [wicked] war with our sister republic." Douglass complained that although many Americans thought the war was wrong, they did not speak out for peace. One newspaper that did speak out was Garrison's

Led by General Scott (center, on horseback), eight thousand American troops routed the Mexican army of thirty thousand men. Here, the general surveys the battle scene.

Liberator. As the Americans neared Mexico City, the paper emphatically stated:

> Every lover of Freedom and humanity, throughout the world, must wish them [the Mexicans] the most triumphant success.... We only hope that, if blood has to flow, that it has been that of the Americans, and that the next news we shall hear will be that General Scott and his army are in the hands of the Mexicans.... We wish him and his troops no bodily harm, but the most utter defeat and disgrace.

Polk and his generals were not swayed by the protests. The president believed that taking Mexico City was essential to a complete victory, which would allow the United States to seize whatever Mexican land it wanted. General Scott had his own reasons for capturing the Mexican capital. He believed that the recognition he would receive would assure him a presidential nomination in the coming election.

Scott reached the seventy-five-hundred-foot-high Valley of Mexico, in the center of which rested Mexico City, in mid-August 1847. His scouts informed him that Santa Anna had heavily fortified the main eastern approach to the city. In addition, they said, there were many lakes and lava beds surrounding the city, so a direct assault would be extremely difficult.

After carefully studying the area, Scott noticed that Santa Anna had once more failed to fortify a strategic area; in this case, the muddy shores of a lake south of the city were left open to

Mexico City, a Natural Fortress

On reaching Mexico City, the attacking American army discovered that capturing the capital would be no easy task. The city of 200,000 people was endowed with many natural defenses. It was located at an altitude of 7,500 feet above sea level in the center of an ancient volcanic crater. The crater was huge, measuring forty-six by thirty-two miles. It was surrounded by rugged mountains containing many strategic spots from which defenders might ambush approaching enemies.

In Aztec days, the area was filled almost entirely with water, and the Indians lived on islands. Over the centuries, the Spanish used rocks and earth to fill in large sections of the great lake. By the time of the war with the United States, the city covered dozens of square miles and was almost completely encircled by six individual lakes. The shores of these lakes were swampy and difficult to cross, forcing would-be attackers to approach the city along narrow, easily defended causeways. General Scott's men, however, managed to travel across the muddy but undefended shore of Lake Chalco. Had Santa Anna fortified this shore area, the Americans would have taken much longer to reach the city.

In this nineteenth-century lithograph, General Scott and his lieutenants ride into the central market area of Mexico City.

attack. The route did appear impassable, but Scott took a chance and ordered his men into the swamp. On August 19, after an exhausting, bug-infested trek, the Americans emerged from the shallows and marched on the city from the south.

Bloody Skirmishes

The troops then engaged in two days of bloody skirmishes outside the city. The Mexicans furiously fought to keep the *yanquis* away, and casualties were heavy. It was now obvious to both Scott and Santa Anna that an all-out assault would cause tremendous losses on both sides. An informal cease-fire took effect, and on August 22, officers from the two armies met and agreed to open negotiations. Santa Anna personally asked former president Herrera, a man he had once helped to throw out of office, to represent Mexico in the talks. The patriotic Herrera accepted the job.

Jose Joaquin Herrera, Man of Peace

One of the finest of Mexico's early presidents, Jose Herrera (1792–1854) was born in the Spanish colony of Guatemala, located directly south of Mexico. This made him a criollo, a person of Spanish descent born in a New World Spanish colony. When Herrera was a child, his family moved to Mexico, where he received an excellent education. He joined the Spanish army in 1809 and quickly rose through the ranks.

Herrera sympathized with the rebels Miguel Hidalgo and Jose Maria Morelos, who wanted to free Mexico of Spanish domination. But Herrera did not join the independence movement until 1821, when he backed Augustin de Iturbide, who became Mexico's first president. When Iturbide declared himself emperor, Herrera was among the leaders who removed him from power and later served his country as minister of war and president of the supreme court. An avowed liberal, he continually opposed the warlike policies of conservatives like Santa Anna.

In 1844, Herrera became president and immediately faced the problem of American annexation of Texas. Though he wanted peace, he was forced to defend the honor of his country and sternly warned the United States to stay out of Texas. He cut off diplomatic relations as soon as Texas became a state but continued to work for peace. When President Polk sent John Slidell to buy New Mexico and California, Herrera gave in to the anti-American sentiments shared by the people of his country and refused to see Slidell. But Herrera's conservative opponents were outraged that he still advocated negotiating with the Americans. Claiming that he had betrayed his country, the conservatives, led by Santa Anna, ousted Herrera from power in January 1846.

After the war, Herrera became president again, serving from 1848 to 1851. He is best remembered for his fairness, dedication to honest government, and courageous efforts to keep his country out of war.

Mexican and American troops engage in battle at Chapultepec. On the hill above them is the ornate palace that once housed Spanish viceroys.

The talks went on for more than ten days but finally broke down. The two sides could not agree on new borders for Mexico. Also, the Mexicans wanted the United States to pay for some of the damages it had caused during the war. Traditionally, it is the loser who pays the winner of a war, not the other way around. In Washington, Polk and the members of his cabinet were outraged. The president ordered Scott to resume hostilities and teach the Mexicans a lesson. One of the bloodiest and most tragic episodes in the history of warfare followed.

On September 10, 1847, the American army approached Chapultepec Hill on the western edge of the capital. A slab of volcanic rock 195 feet high and 600 yards long, Chapultepec overlooked the wide causeways that led to the heart of the city. At the summit of the hill stood an ornate palace, once the home of the Spanish viceroys. Now the building housed the National Military Academy, Mexico's version of West Point. These were the famed "Halls of Montezuma," named after the Aztec ruler of pre-Spanish days. The place was more than a national landmark. It was a symbol of a proud Mexican heritage. In the eyes of the

Mexicans, Chapultepec *was* Mexico. Scott knew that if he could take the hill, then the city would be his, both strategically and symbolically.

A Deadly Barrage

Two days later, on September 12, at 9:00 A.M., the American cannons began firing on the hill and the city beyond. Row after row of artillery continued the deadly barrage all day and into the night. Buildings crumbled, and the screams of dying people echoed through the city streets. One shopkeeper later wrote, "In some cases whole blocks were destroyed and a great number of men, women and children killed and wounded."

The next morning, at precisely 8:00, the artillery bombardment ceased, and thousands of American infantry advanced on the hill. Gen. William Worth led a force toward the north side of the palace, while Col. Gideon Pillow's men attacked from the southwest. Waiting for them behind the tall concrete retaining walls that encircled the palace was the Mexican general Nicolas Bravo. He had only eleven hundred men, for Santa Anna had decided to keep the rest of the army inside the city walls. About eight hundred of Bravo's soldiers were seasoned troops. The rest were cadets from the academy, thirteen- and fourteen-year-old boys in pressed gray uniforms and bright blue hats with tassels. The defenders knew that they were all that stood between the yanquis and the city. They would be defending their homes, their religion, and their way of life. Grimly, they watched the waves of American soldiers roll toward them.

As Pillow's men reached the walls, the Mexicans opened fire. Dozens of American cannons answered back, blasting many of the Mexicans to pieces. The Americans brought up scaling ladders and scurried up the massive walls. Some used crowbars and hatchets to cut handholds in the walls. The Mexicans repeatedly fired volleys into the faces of the Americans who reached the top, and blood began to soak the dirt at the base of the hill. When the defenders ran out of bullets, they swung their muskets like clubs and tried to beat away the attackers. As the Americans finally swarmed over the summit of the hill, there was savage hand-to-hand fighting. The cadets valiantly held their ground in the massacre that followed. In the space of only a few minutes, the Americans shot, stabbed, and hacked to death nearly all of Bravo's forces.

The Boy Heroes

The last six Mexicans left alive were cadets, who rushed to prevent the Americans from capturing and defiling the Mexican flag. In a dramatic gesture, one of the boys wrapped himself in his

The Monument to the Boy Heroes

At the entrance to the park on Chapultepec Hill in Mexico City stands Mexico's most revered national shrine. It is the monument that pays tribute to *Los Niños Heroes* (the Boy Heroes). They were the cadets of Mexico's National Military Academy who gallantly gave their lives during the battle for the city in the Mexican-American War.

When the Americans stormed Chapultepec on September 13, 1847, the thirteen- and fourteen-year-old cadets fought to the last man alongside the regular Mexican troops. At the end of the battle, cadet Juan Escutia wrapped himself in the Mexican flag. He and his five remaining companions shouted, *Viva Mexico! Viva el Colegio Militar!* (Long live Mexico! Long live the military academy!). Then they leaped to their deaths from the towers of the academy.

The sacrifice of *Los Niños* is often celebrated in Mexican books, paintings, sculptures, and films. Each year, on September 13, the anniversary of the battle, the president of Mexico awards swords to present-day cadets in honor of the fallen heroes. On that day, thousands of people make pilgrimages to the monument.

In March 1947, President Harry S Truman visited Mexico. For many Mexicans, the high point of his tour was the moment he placed a wreath of flowers on the monument to *Los Niños*. It was an American gesture of regret over an unfortunate war and a remembrance of one of the most courageous moments ever to occur in battle.

Six young Mexican cadets leapt to their deaths after the battle of Chapultepec (below).

country's colors. Then, shouting, "Long live Mexico!" he threw himself over the towering walls. Rather than surrender, his five comrades also jumped to their deaths. Later generations of Mexicans would proudly remember the cadets as *Los Niños Heroes* (the Boy Heroes).

As the Americans ran up their own flag on Chapultepec Hill, the news came that Santa Anna had fled the city with his last few thousand troops. The battle was over and so was the war. Thousands of people were dead, and many thousands more were wounded, homeless, or orphaned. With bitterness, the survivors crawled from the ruins and began to pick up the pieces of their lives and their country. These were the war's other victims—the everyday citizens of Mexico City, Vera Cruz, Monterrey, and the dozens of towns and villages devastated by the fighting. They would have no say when the leaders met to work out the terms of surrender and determine the all-important matter of new borders for the two nations. Territory, after all, was what the fighting had been all about.

CHAPTER SEVEN

The Victor Is the Vanquished –The Treaty Is Signed

General Santa Anna, once considered a great warrior by his countrymen, is exiled in disgrace to Jamaica after the Mexican-American War.

I n October 1847, President Polk sent American diplomat Nicholas P. Trist to help General Scott negotiate a treaty with the Mexicans. But the two men had to wait for the Mexican government to reorganize itself. During the confusion and hysteria of the final assault on the capital, the government had, more or less, fallen apart. Santa Anna had resigned both the presidency and command of the army. The Mexican people later exiled him in disgrace to the island of Jamaica in the Caribbean Sea. After the fall of Mexico, there was no Mexican head of state to meet with the Americans.

With the Mexican leadership in disarray, the army decimated, and the country in a state of disorder, it would have been easy for the Americans to take over all of Mexico. Trist and Scott were aware of this. In fact, there was a great deal of popular sentiment in the United States for doing so. The All Mexico movement had become powerful during the last months of the war. Leaders of the movement felt that the war prizes of New Mexico and the ports of California were not enough. If the Americans controlled Mexico, they could construct a canal across the narrowest portion of the country. This would allow Americans to travel from the Atlantic Ocean into the Pacific without having to sail all the way around South America. Travel time by boat to California would be dramatically reduced.

But American leaders, even the expansionist Polk, were reluctant to make Mexico a part of the United States. For one thing, it would be difficult and expensive to govern a non-English-speaking

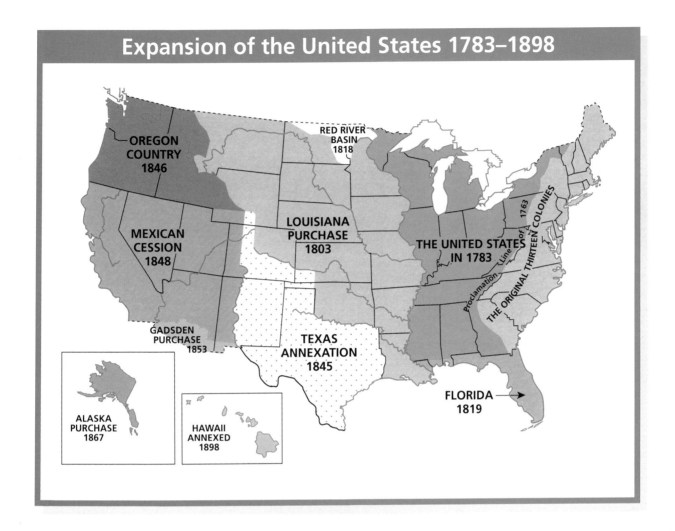

Expansion of the United States 1783–1898

OREGON COUNTRY 1846

RED RIVER BASIN 1818

MEXICAN CESSION 1848

LOUISIANA PURCHASE 1803

THE UNITED STATES IN 1783

Proclamation Line of 1763

THE ORIGINAL THIRTEEN COLONIES

GADSDEN PURCHASE 1853

TEXAS ANNEXATION 1845

FLORIDA 1819

ALASKA PURCHASE 1867

HAWAII ANNEXED 1898

people who were formed by a very different culture and set of traditions. Racism also played a part in the decision. Many Americans saw the Mexicans as inferiors who might intermarry with Anglos and "pollute" the white race.

Some, including Trist and Scott, felt that the most important reason for allowing Mexico its freedom was to uphold American ideals. The United States itself, they said, had been born out of a fight for freedom and should not impose itself on other peoples. Newspaper editor John O'Sullivan said that the United States must "never admit within its own Union those who do not freely desire the boon."

A Treaty Is Signed

And so, Trist and Scott waited patiently for the Mexicans to put their country in order. Eventually, the popular patriot Manuel de la Peña y Peña assumed the role of temporary president and met

The United States Expands

The 1848 Treaty of Guadalupe Hidalgo increased the size of the United States by nearly one-third. The agreement gave the United States the Mexican provinces of California and New Mexico. This vast territory included the future states of California, Nevada, and Utah as well as sections of Arizona, New Mexico, Wyoming, and Colorado. Millions of acres of prairies, mountain ranges, deserts, and fertile valleys were now open to American settlement and development. These lands brought the country a wealth of natural resources. Valuable metals and minerals, as well as vast oil riches, were later found in former Mexican territories. Only one year after the end of the war, a huge gold rush drew thousands of people to California.

The country now stretched from the Atlantic to the Pacific Ocean. U.S. control of the excellent California ports of San Francisco, Los Angeles, and San Diego extended American influence into the Pacific sphere. It also opened up valuable trade routes with Japan, China, and other Asian nations. Thus, the American defeat of Mexico was an important factor in the United States' eventual rise to the status of the world's wealthiest nation.

with the Americans. After months of negotiations, the American and Mexican representatives agreed on a treaty. They signed it on February 2, 1848, in the town of Guadalupe Hidalgo. The U.S. Senate ratified the document on March 10, the newly elected Mexican Congress on May 25.

It came as no surprise that the treaty granted the huge territories of California and New Mexico to the United States. The treaty also established once and for all that the Rio Grande was the southern border of Texas. Another term of the treaty, however, was somewhat of a surprise. The United States was to pay Mexico fifteen million dollars for the ceded territories and to help rebuild the country. This agreement outraged conservatives in the United States. Why, they asked, should the winner of the conflict pay the loser? It normally happened the other way around. And had not American leaders rejected the very same notion before attacking Mexico City? Many called for rejecting the treaty.

When the war ended, military men returned to their homes. Here, an American sailor is reunited with his wife.

In this 1845 engraving from Illustrated London News, *Americans fire artillery and guns to celebrate the nearing of the end of the Mexican-American War.*

But supporters of the treaty pointed out that Mexico was totally bankrupt and incapable of paying reparations or compensation for damages to the United States. And, they insisted, it would ensure better future relations between the two nations if the United States showed generosity. While some people continued to grumble about the money, most Americans came out in support of the treaty. One newspaper editor declared, "Admit all [the treaty's] faults and say if an aimless and endless foreign war is not far worse…. We are glad to get out of the scrape even upon these terms."

Greed for Land

There were people on both sides of the Rio Grande who felt that the United States had given away more than money to Mexico. Although the war had been a decisive military victory for the

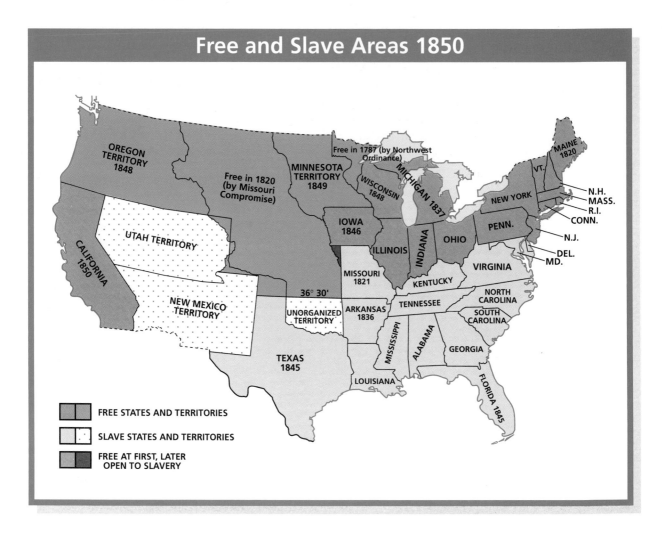

Free and Slave Areas 1850

OREGON TERRITORY 1848

Free in 1820 (by Missouri Compromise)

MINNESOTA TERRITORY 1849

Free in 1787 (by Northwest Ordinance)

MICHIGAN 1837

WISCONSIN 1848

MAINE 1820

VT.

NEW YORK

N.H.
MASS.
R.I.
CONN.

UTAH TERRITORY

CALIFORNIA 1850

IOWA 1846

ILLINOIS

INDIANA

OHIO

PENN.

N.J.

DEL.
MD.

VIRGINIA

MISSOURI 1821

KENTUCKY

NEW MEXICO TERRITORY

36° 30'

UNORGANIZED TERRITORY

ARKANSAS 1836

TENNESSEE

NORTH CAROLINA

SOUTH CAROLINA

MISSISSIPPI

ALABAMA

GEORGIA

TEXAS 1845

LOUISIANA

FLORIDA 1845

FREE STATES AND TERRITORIES

SLAVE STATES AND TERRITORIES

FREE AT FIRST, LATER OPEN TO SLAVERY

United States, many people felt that it had been a moral defeat. And, in a way, the victor was really the vanquished. According to this view, held by Abraham Lincoln, Joshua Giddings, and Frederick Douglass as well as by many Mexican leaders, the United States had purposely provoked a war with a hopelessly weaker nation. And it had done so out of greed for land.

The American Anti-Slavery Society added another motive, saying the war was "waged solely for the detestable and horrible purpose of extending and perpetuating American slavery throughout the vast territory of Mexico." The poet James Russell Lowell also felt the war had morally weakened the United States. He spoke of the American desire to plunder Mexico in order to get California and other riches. Using the dialect of a New England farmer, he wrote in the *Boston Courier:*

> Ez fer war, I call it murder—
> There you hev it plain an' flat;
> I don't want to go no furder
> Than my Testyment for that.

Others opposed to the war insisted that it had been far more unpopular in the United States than Polk had claimed. They pointed to record numbers of desertions from army ranks during the fighting. And fewer men had actually volunteered than the government contended. Some reported being forced into military service. James Miller of Norfolk, Virginia, wrote of being "dragged aboard of a boat landed at Fort Monroe, and closely immured in the guard house for sixteen days." Others said they were offered three months pay in advance if they signed up but never saw the money. Enlisting in the army eventually became so unpopular that in 1847, Congress promised one hundred acres of public land to any man who stayed in the service long enough to receive an honorable discharge.

Victory as Poison

One of the most serious criticisms of the fighting was that the war had blemished the reputation of the United States as a fair and peace-loving nation. The poet Ralph Waldo Emerson had earlier predicted that the United States would easily defeat Mexico. But he added that the victory would "poison us." For the first time in its history, he said, the United States would gain a world image as a militaristic power. It would become like England, Spain, France, and other European countries—imperialistic, seeking to extend its influence and build an empire at the expense of weaker peoples.

The widely read *Whig Intelligencer* suggested that the fifteen million dollars paid to Mexico was a ploy used to draw attention away from the use of naked force in gaining Mexican lands. The United States had paid for the land fair and square, the paper humorously quipped. Therefore, it added, "we take nothing by conquest.... Thank God."

All these antiwar criticisms were, of course, quite unofficial. The official viewpoint of the U.S. government was the one introduced by Polk in his declaration of war. The United States, he said, rightfully avenged the killing of Americans on American land. From the Mexican viewpoint, the United States was the aggressor. The Mexicans felt that they fought gallantly against impossible odds. They physically lost the war, they admitted, but morally defeated the United States. During the decades that followed, as the two countries became friends and trading partners, these sharply different impressions of the same events remained fundamentally unchanged. They remain so to this day.

A Training Ground for Future Leaders

Many of the United States' future presidents and military generals served in the Mexican-American War. Zachary Taylor, one of the two principal generals of the war (along with Winfield Scott), was elected president in 1848 but died in office in 1850. Franklin Pierce, who commanded twenty-four hundred troops in the war and fought in the battle for Mexico City, became the fourteenth president of the United States serving from 1853 to 1857. Jefferson Davis fought under Taylor at the Battle of Buena Vista in 1847. Davis became president of the Confederate States of America during the Civil War (1861–1865). Capt. Robert E. Lee was an army engineer who played a crucial role in the victory over Santa Anna at Cerro Gordo. Later, as a general, Lee led the armies of the Confederacy against his old friend Ulysses S. Grant. Lieutenant Grant served under Taylor in Texas and northern Mexico. After leading the Union Army during the Civil War, he served two terms as president, holding office from 1869 to 1877.

How much their experience in the Mexican-American War helped these men become leaders is uncertain. But it is interesting to note that so many participated in the war.

Glossary

adobe   bricks of sun-dried mud used to construct crude buildings.

Anglos   white Americans.

annexation   the joining of two territories as one territory becomes incorporated into the other.

artillery   cannons or other large, powerful guns.

bowie knife   weapon designed by frontiersman Jim Bowie. The knife has a huge, wide blade, the back edge of which is curved and sharpened to a point.

cavalry   troops mounted on horses.

criollos   people born in Mexico of Spanish descent.

deguello   Mexican bugle call signifying that no mercy is to be given to the enemy.

expansionism   the doctrine that promotes increasing a country's size by constantly acquiring new lands.

flanking movement   military maneuver that allows an army to attack the extreme left or right sides of the enemy's position.

flintlock   or musket, a primitive rifle that works by inserting both powder and projectile directly into the barrel of the weapon.

garrison   a group of soldiers at a military outpost.

grachupines   Mexican citizens born in Spain.

heresy   the expression of an idea contrary to the doctrines of the Catholic church.

imperialistic   seeking to extend a country's influence and power at the expense of weaker peoples.

infantry   foot soldiers.

lancers   mounted soldiers armed with lances, or long spears.

manifest destiny the doctrine claiming that the United States was fated by God to expand from the Atlantic to the Pacific Ocean.

mestizos people born of marriages between Mexicans and local Indians.

reparations money or goods given to one country by another as payment for damages inflicted during war.

republic a country whose government is elected by the people.

siesta a Spanish custom of napping, or resting, in the afternoon.

vanguard the frontmost units of an army.

viceroy the governor of a Spanish colony who reports directly to the king of Spain.

For Further Reading

Donald Barr Chidsey, *The War with Mexico*. New York: Crown, 1968.

Ellis Cradle, *Mexico, Land of Hidden Treasure*. Camden, NJ: Thomas Nelson & Sons, 1967.

Fairfax Downey, *Texas and the War with Mexico*. New York: American Heritage Publishing, 1961.

Marion Gartler and George L. Hall, *Understanding Mexico*. River Forest, IL: Laidlaw Brothers, 1964.

Robert Leckie, *Great American Battles*. New York: Random House, 1968.

David Nevin, *The Texans*. New York: Time-Life Books, 1975.

Lon Tinkle, *The Alamo*. New York: New American Library, 1958.

Works Consulted

Karl J. Bauer, *The Mexican War*. New York: MacMillan, 1974.

William Campbell Blinkley, *The Expansionist Movement in Texas*. Berkeley: University of California Press, 1925.

Isaac George, *Heroes and Incidents of the Mexican War*. San Bernardino, CA: Borgo Press, 1982.

Michael C. Meyer and William L. Sherman, *The Course of Mexican History*. New York: Oxford University Press, 1983.

Henry Banford Parkes, *A History of Mexico*. Boston: Houghton Mifflin, 1960.

Charles L. Sanford, ed., *Manifest Destiny and the Imperialism Question*. New York: John Wiley & Sons, 1974.

John H. Schroeder, *Mr. Polk's War*. Madison: University of Wisconsin Press, 1973.

Nathaniel W. Stephenson, *Texas and the Mexican War*. New Haven, CT: Yale University Press, 1921.

Irwin Unger, *These United States, the Questions of Our Past*. Boston: Little, Brown, 1978.

Howard Zinn, *A People's History of the United States*. New York: Harper & Row, 1980.

Index

Photo Credits

Cover photo: Library of Congress

Adams, John Quincy, by Pieter van Huffel, National Portrait Gallery, Smithsonian Institution, 41 (left)

The Daughters of the Republic of Texas Library, 17, 18, 22 (right), 24 (both), 26 (bottom), 27 (all), 28, 33, 34, 35, 43 (top)

The Eugene C. Barker Texas History Center, The University of Texas, Austin, 32 (left), 43 (bottom)

Frost Publishing Group, Ltd., 39

Institute of Texan Cultures, The University of Texas at San Antonio, 10, 11, 12 (left, right, and center), 15 (both), 26 (top), 32 (right), 40, 42 (left), 47 (top and center), 56 (top), 59 (top), 71

Jackson, Andrew, by James Barton Longacre, National Portrait Gallery, Smithsonian Institution, 41 (middle)

Library of Congress, 6, 7, 9, 14 (both), 20, 21, 22 (left and center), 23, 25, 29 (both), 46, 47 (left), 48, 51 (both), 53, 55, 57, 58 (both), 59 (center and bottom), 61, 62, 63, 64 (both), 65, 66, 67 (both), 70, 72 (both), 73, 74 (all), 75, 76, 78, 79, 80, 82, 84, 85

Taylor, Zachary, attributed to James Reid Lambdin, National Portrait Gallery, Smithsonian Institution, 52

Texas State Library, Austin, 42 (right)

Thoreau, Henry David, by Benjamin D. Maxham, National Portrait Gallery, Smithsonian Institution, 56 (bottom)

Van Buren, Martin, by John Langendoerffer, National Portrait Gallery, Smithsonian Institution, 41 (right)

About the Author

Don Nardo is an award-winning writer. He has also worked before or behind the camera in twenty films. Several of his musical compositions, including a young person's version of *The War of the Worlds* and the oratorio *Richard III*, have been played by regional orchestras. Mr. Nardo's writing credits include short stories, articles, and more than twenty books, including *Lasers: Humanity's Magic Light; Anxiety and Phobias; The Irish Potato Famine; Exercise; and Gravity: The Universal Force*. Among his other writings are an episode of ABC's "Spenser: For Hire" and numerous screenplays. Mr. Nardo lives with his wife, Christine, on Cape Cod, Massachusetts.

SPACE
Disasters

Rob Alcraft

Heinemann Library
Chicago, Illinois

© 2000 Reed Educational & Professional Publishing
Published by Heinemann Library
an imprint of Reed Educational & Professional Publishing,
100 N. LaSalle, Suite 1010
Chicago, IL 60602

Customer Service 888-454-2279

Designed by Celia Floyd
Illustrations by David Cuzik (Pennant Illustration)
Originated by Dot Gradations
Printed by Wing King Tong, in Hong Kong

04 03 02 01 00
10 9 8 7 6 5 4 3 2 1

Library of Congress Cataloging-in-Publication Data
Alcraft, Rob, 1966-
      Space disasters / Rob Alcraft.
            p. cm. – (World's worst)
      Includes bibliographical references and index.
      Summary: Examines the events leading to the Apollo 13 explosion,
   failed Soyuz 11 mission, and the Challenger disaster, the
   consequences of these accidents, and how they might have been
   averted.
   ISBN 1-57572-992-X
   1. Space vehicle accidents Juvenile works. [1. Space vehicle
accidents.] I. Title. II. Series.
   TL553.5.A54 1999
   363.12'4—dc21   99-34943
                                                              CIP

Acknowledgments
The Publishers would like to thank the following for permission to reproduce photographs:
Image Select, pp. 4, 21; Novosti, p. 5; Planet Earth Pictures, pp.7, 8, 24, 25; NASA, pp. 6, 9, 12, 13, 20, 27; Novosti (London), pp. 14, 15, 18, 19, 29; ; Tony Stone/IM House, p. 26; Science Photo Library/Mark Paternostro, p. 28.

Cover photograph reproduced with permission of NASA/Science Photo Library

Every effort has been made to contact copyright holders of any material reproduced in this book. Any omissions will be rectified in subsequent printings if notice is given to the Publisher.

Some words are shown in bold, **like this**. You can find out what they mean by looking in the glossary

Contents

The Journey into Space

Space travel has become part of our lives. We take it for granted. Today, **satellites** and rockets are launched almost as a matter of routine. Perhaps we have forgotten how amazing and dangerous space travel really is. Within the lifetime of your grandparents, it was thought that space travel was an impossible dream. Even if we could get a human into space, no one was sure what would happen to them when they got there.

James Irwin, from the *Apollo 15* mission, stands on the moon's surface and salutes the U.S. flag.

In 1961, the **USSR** launched the *Vostok 1*. Inside was Yuri Gagarin, the first person in space. He made one **orbit** around the earth. Despite fears about what would happen, he landed safely. Within three years, the first **space walk** was safely completed. Four years later, in 1969, the U.S. *Apollo 7* mission landed Neil Armstrong and Edwin "Buzz" Aldrin on the moon. It seemed to many people that space had been conquered. But the risks remained.

Along with the successes, there have also been disasters. In this book, we'll look at three of the worst disasters in the history of space exploration. We will look at the technology and the dangers of space travel. What could have been done to prevent disaster? Who, if anyone, was to blame?

Laika was sent up in a **pressurized** cabin in *Sputnik 2*. Because they did not have a way of bringing her safely back to Earth, scientists put her to sleep by remote control after a week in space.

Animals in space

The first test pilots for manned space flight were monkeys and dogs. In the 1950s, both the USSR and the U.S. used them to test the effects of space on living things. The first living being to make it from Earth into space was a dog named Laika. Laika blasted off into space aboard the Russian *Sputnik 2* on November 3, 1957.

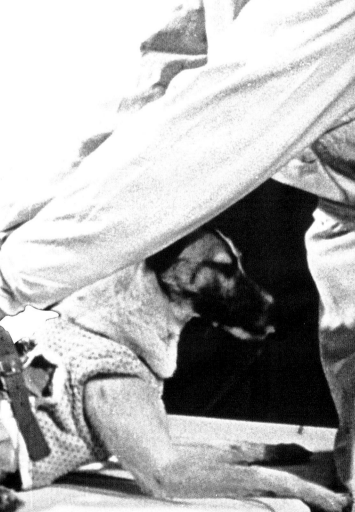

Reaching for the Stars

Space is a dangerous place. Even getting there is dangerous. Space rockets are really no more than huge fireworks that can, if things go wrong, explode.

Ordinary jet engines are not powerful enough to produce the huge thrust a spacecraft needs to escape Earth's **gravity**. Instead, a space rocket burns oxygen and hydrogen. Both gases are extremely explosive. Many rockets have not even made it off the **launch pad**. Their fuel tanks have simply exploded.

When a space rocket reaches space, there are even more dangers. Space is a **vacuum**. There is no air, and it is very cold. A spacecraft must carry everything astronauts need to survive—even the air they need to breathe! Spacecraft must be completely sealed off from the outside. Even a tiny leak of air alters the air pressure. As a result, the astronauts die.

This is what the earth looks like from space. Pictures like this are familiar today, but before space travel, no one had ever seen what the earth looked like.

Dangers and risks

Another dangerous part of the space journey is **re-entry**—when the spacecraft plunges back into the earth's **atmosphere**. The **friction** between the spacecraft and the atmosphere makes temperatures soar to almost 3000°F (1600°C). **Satellites** and **meteorites** burn up in the atmosphere before they reach the ground. A spacecraft needs to get through the atmosphere intact if its crew is to survive.

There have been more than 207 manned space missions. Given the risks, it is amazing that so few have ended in disaster. Even small mistakes can bring tragic results.

Lift-off!

The European *Ariane* rocket is 188 feet (57 meters) high and can lift a load of 4 tons into an **orbit** 240 miles (400 kilometers) above the earth. *Ariane*—like most rocket systems—uses three stages to escape Earth's gravity.

1. Lift-off: the powerful liquid-fuel engines and **booster rockets** light. At 36 miles (60 kilometers) up, the booster rockets run out of fuel. They separate and float to Earth by parachute.

2. Next, the main engine fires and burns. This engine then falls away and burns up on re-entry.

3. The final-stage rocket fires, propelling *Ariane* to around 17,280 miles (28,800 kilometers) per hour, fast enough to leave the earth's atmosphere, and into the planned orbit.

Ariane 4 took off on its first flight in June 1988. It was carrying satellites.

7

Explosion!
Near Disaster for Apollo 13

Apollo 13 took off on April 11, 1970. The mission of the astronauts—John L. Swigert, Fred W. Haise Jr., and Captain James Lovell—was to land on the moon. But they never got there. On April 13, an explosion on board left the men fighting for survival.

A good start

At 1:13 P.M. on April 11, 1970, *Apollo 13* was launched. It had three different rocket stages. After each stage did its job, it was **jettisoned**. Three more stages entered space. The **Service Module** was packed with equipment. The **Command Module** (*Odyssey*) was the astronauts' home for the journey. The **Lunar Module** (*Aquarius*) was to take two men down to the moon.

Forty-six hours into the flight, the commander at the Kennedy Space Center joked to the astronauts: "The spacecraft is in real good shape as far as we are concerned. We're bored to tears down here." There was even time for a TV broadcast of the crew showing life in **weightless** space.

All appeared to be going well as *Apollo 13*, powered by a Saturn 5 rocket, blasted off for its journey to the moon.

8

Emergency in space

Then, after just 56 hours in space, oxygen tank number two suddenly exploded. Tank one also failed. Inside the Command Module, warning lights flashed. Then, one after the other, all power, light, and heat systems failed. The three astronauts were 200,000 miles (320,000 kilometers) from home. The oxygen supply was running out. If something was not done, the astronauts would die.

Captain James Lovell, from the *Apollo 13* mission, listens during training.

Captain James Lovell, speaking after the event:

When you first hear this explosion or bang...you don't know what it is. Then I looked out of the window and saw this **venting***. My concern was increasing all the time. I went from "I wonder what this is going to do to the landing" to "I wonder if we can get back home again" and when I looked up and saw both oxygen pressures...one actually at zero and the other one going down...it dawned on me that we were in serious trouble.*

"Houston, we have a problem."

Deep in space, Lovell peered out of the window. He could see a thin cloud of gas boiling out into space. It was making the spacecraft spin wildly. *Apollo 13* was in serious trouble.

1. On April 13, 1970, at 55 hours and 55 minutes into the *Apollo 13* mission, an oxygen tank explodes. A second tank is damaged and its oxygen lost. The craft's **fuel cells** begin to fail—they need oxygen to work.

2. On Earth, experts realize it is too dangerous to use the main engine on the **Service Module**. But the smaller engine on the **Lunar Module** does not have enough power to turn *Apollo* around. The only option is to use the pull of the moon's **gravity** to "swing" *Apollo 13* back towards Earth.

3. An hour later, the crew of *Apollo 13* decides to abandon the **Command Module**. It only has enough power and oxygen left to last through **re-entry**. They enter the Lunar Module. It is designed to keep two men alive for 45 hours. Now it must keep three men alive for 84 hours. To survive, they build a makeshift air filter. This will allow them to breathe for the extra hours.

4. Mission Control decides to try two burns of the Lunar Module engine—one to put *Apollo 13* on the right course and one to speed it on its way. Sixty hours into the mission, the crew does the first engine burn, for 35 seconds.

5. Almost 76½ hours into the mission, *Apollo 13* passes behind the moon. For 25 minutes, it is out of radio contact with Earth. The crew makes a second engine burn for five minutes, but *Apollo 13* drifts off course. At 128 hours and 31 minutes into the mission, the descent engine is fired to slow the craft down and to make sure it hits the earth's atmosphere at the right angle.

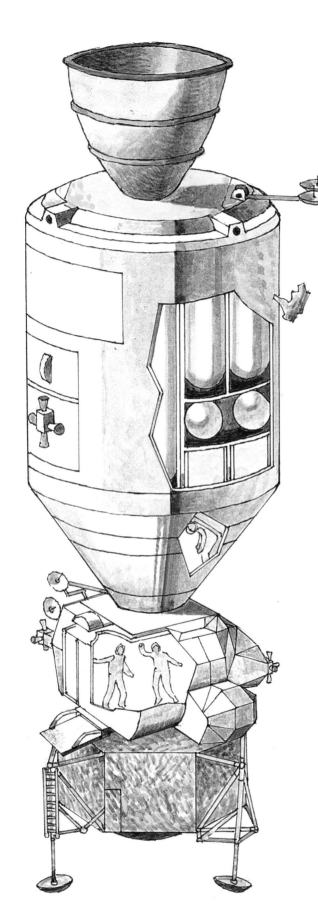

6. On April 17, Lunar Module systems are switched on again. Four hours before splash down, the crew **jettisons** the Service Module. As it drifts away, they can see that one side had been completely blown off. At 90 minutes before re-entry, the crew enters the Command Module and jettisons the Lunar Module. Will the Command Module's heat shield withstand the incredible heat of re-entry? For three and a half minutes, during re-entry, there is silence.

Splash Down

Apollo 13 made it home. The heat shield worked and the crew was alive. But what had gone wrong to cause this disaster? The investigations showed how even small errors can lead to potentially big disasters.

Apollo 13 parachuted safely into the sea. The astronauts arrived home to a great welcome.

Engineer detectives

A team of **NASA** engineers tracked the history of the defective oxygen tank and tested their theories on an identical tank. They discovered that oxygen tank number two, which exploded, had been damaged while it was being made. They also found that when both tanks were redesigned, the **thermostatic** switches that controlled the temperature were not changed.

Before the launch, the oxygen tanks were tested. During this testing, **Teflon** insulation on electrical wires inside tank number two was damaged. This damage went unnoticed until things went wrong during the mission. The faulty wires caused sparks and an explosion. The fate of *Apollo 13* was sealed before it even left the ground.

Lessons learned

NASA's careful investigations led to recommendations to improve safety on future missions. These included the instruction that whenever even slight problems occur with systems before a launch, the history of that instrument or part should be carefully studied before it is used.

NASA also decided that oxgyen storage systems should be altered to reduce the risk of fire—by minimizing the use of Teflon and other **combustible** materials. NASA also reviewed what food and emergency equipment should be kept in the **Command Module** or other "extra" modules for an emergency.

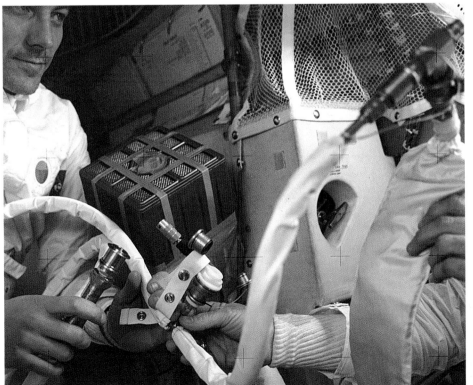

In order to breathe in the **Lunar Module,** the crew of *Apollo 13* had to make an emergency air filter from materials on board.

Disaster!
The End of the Soyuz 11 Mission

On June 29, 1971, the **Command Module** of the **USSR's** *Soyuz 11* spacecraft was recovered in Kazakhstan. A hero's welcome was planned. But inside the capsule, the crew was dead.

The longest mission

The USSR launched the world's first space station, called *Salyut 1*, on April 19, 1971. It was a floating laboratory. On board were more than 1,300 instruments, including a tiny "farm."

Soyuz 11 was designed to carry scientists up to the space station. It was launched on June 6, 1971. At first, it seemed a total success. The three **cosmonauts** on board *Soyuz 11* boarded the space station without problems. For 22 days, the crew completed scientific experiments and studied the surface of Earth and its weather and cloud formations. The cosmonauts studied how their bodies reacted to **weightlessness**.

Soyuz 11 was launched successfully on its mission to the *Salyut 1* space station. But the three cosmonauts on board died on **re-entry** 23 days later.

On June 24, they had beaten the record for the longest space flight. Television pictures of the crew were beamed across the USSR. The cosmonauts become national heroes as they somersaulted across the screens of millions of viewers. Yet when they returned they were unable to enjoy the hero's welcome prepared for them. On June 29, 1971, as *Soyuz 11* re-entered the earth's **atmosphere**, the three men died.

Penguin suits

Because there is no **gravity** in space, many of the muscles that are essential on Earth grow weak and flabby. The three cosmonauts on *Soyuz 11* wore special elastic suits, nicknamed "penguin suits." The suits made the men work hard to move their muscles. It was as if they were constantly lifting weights!

Viktor Patsayev
Profession: engineer
Born: June 19, 1933
Missions flown: 1

Georgi Dobrovolsky (Commander)
Profession: pilot
Born: June 1, 1928
Missions flown: 1

Vladislav Volkov
Profession: engineer
Born: Nov. 23, 1935
Missions flown: 2

No Hero's Welcome

When the deaths of the three **cosmonauts** were announced, world leaders and space experts sent messages to the **USSR** expressing their sadness. George Low, the deputy director of **NASA**, said, "Our hearts go out to their families and to their colleagues." Everyone wanted to know what had happened.

1. The *Soyuz 11* mission begins on June 6, 1971. *Soyuz 11* enters **orbit** nine minutes after launch. At 10:50 **GMT** it is circling 135 miles (217 kilometers) above the earth. At this orbit it approaches the *Salyut 1* space station. On June 7, at 07:24 GMT, docking begins. The ship steers automatically until it is within 330 feet (100 meters) of the space station. Then Dobrovolsky takes the controls for docking. Later that day, the crew enters the space station.

2. On June 29, the crew of *Soyuz 11* close up the *Salyut 1* space station. At 18:28 GMT they set off for Earth. **Retro-fire** is complete at 22:35 GMT. "This is Yantar 1," says Dobrovolsky, giving his call sign. "Everything is satisfactory on board. Our condition is excellent. We are ready to land." Next, the three parts of the *Soyuz 11* separate—explosive bolts sending the **Service Module** and **Orbital Module** away from the **Command Module**. There is no more radio contact.

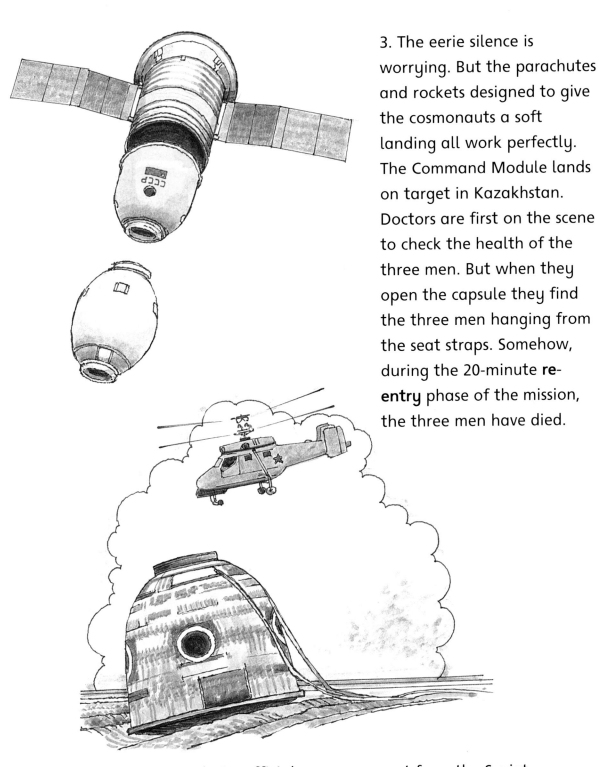

3. The eerie silence is worrying. But the parachutes and rockets designed to give the cosmonauts a soft landing all work perfectly. The Command Module lands on target in Kazakhstan. Doctors are first on the scene to check the health of the three men. But when they open the capsule they find the three men hanging from the seat straps. Somehow, during the 20-minute **re-entry** phase of the mission, the three men have died.

4. An official announcement from the Soviet authorities says "...a helicopter-borne recovery group, upon opening the hatch, found the *Soyuz 11* crew in their seats without any signs of life. The causes of the crew's death are being investigated."

The Missing Minutes

What had happened between the last message from Commander Dobrovolsky and the silent landing in Kazakhstan? In Moscow, the capital of the **USSR**, a special commission was set up to find out. Headed by Mstislav Keldysh, the President of the USSR's Academy of Sciences, the commission talked to the experts responsible for the *Soyuz* mission.

Around the world, experts tried to guess the cause of the disaster. Many thought that the heat shield that was meant to keep the **Command Module** cool as it plummeted back to Earth had failed. In Moscow, people close to those who ran the *Soyuz 11* mission were saying that a hatch had not been closed. The air in the Command Module had leaked out and the **cosmonauts** had died.

The *Soyuz 9* mission pictured here had a happy ending. However, when the *Soyuz 11* command module was opened, the deaths of the three crew members were discovered.

On July 11, 1971, Mstislav Keldysh reported the commission's findings. The disaster was due to a "rapid pressure drop occurring inside the descent vehicle." Few other details were given. The Soviet authorities didn't want to give anyone else useful information. They didn't like to admit mistakes in public.

It took two years before the complete facts about *Soyuz 11* were made public. The disaster had been caused by the shock of the explosive bolts that separated the three stages of *Soyuz 11* just before **re-entry**. The bolts firing had caused a **valve** to open. The valve should not have opened until just before touchdown. Instead, the valve had opened in space, letting all the air out.

No more short cuts

The most important lesson of the *Soyuz 11* disaster was this: when it came to space travel, nothing could be left to chance. The designers of the *Soyuz* craft thought that the cosmonauts did not need **pressure suits**. It was this short cut that killed the three men. When *Soyuz 12* was launched in 1973, only two men were on board. There would be room for pressure suits.

The *Soyuz* disaster also spelled the end for the *Salyut 1* space station. With no safe way of sending men to work on it, it was steered back towards Earth. After 175 days in space, it burned up in the atmosphere over the Pacific Ocean.

Important lessons were learned from *Soyuz 11*. The cosmonauts on board *Soyuz 12* were equipped with pressure suits.

Fireball!
The Challenger Space Shuttle Disaster

On January 28, 1986, a U.S. space shuttle, *Challenger*, prepared for launch. Lift-off seemed to go well. But just 73 seconds after lift-off, *Challenger* exploded in flames.

Explosion in Florida

It was the 25th shuttle mission. U.S. astronauts had launched and returned safely 50 times in 25 years of space flight and exploration. Launches had become so routine that only one TV network was filming it. Yet on the ground at Cape Canaveral in Florida, things were less than routine. Already there had been three launch postponements. Then on January 27, as the astronauts were being strapped in for lift-off, high winds and a broken handle on a hatch caused the launch to be called off—again.

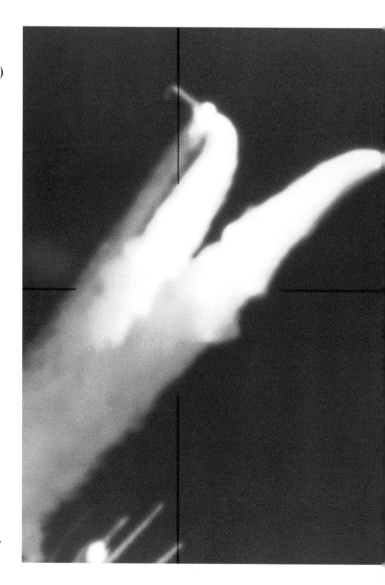

Just 73 seconds after lift-off, the *Challenger* exploded in a giant fireball.

20

On the night of January 27, the temperature dropped unusually low for Florida. Early in the morning, engineers removed icicles from the launch tower. At Mission Control, team members argued about whether or not to go ahead with the launch—the effects of the cold weather on the shuttle were unknown. The predicted launch temperature of 29°F (−1.7°C) was far below the coldest launch so far. But at 11:38 A.M., the launch went ahead anyway.

Challenger rose into the clear Florida sky. Fifty seconds later, the shuttle broke the **sound barrier** and continued to accelerate. Mission Control sent the expected signal, "Challenger, go at throttle up." Sixty-eight seconds into the flight, Commander Dick Scobee gave the response, "Roger, go at throttle up." Seven seconds later, *Challenger* exploded into a giant fireball.

Obviously a major malfunction...the vehicle has exploded.

Steve Nesbitt, a member of the Cape Canaveral control team, tracking the flight on a computer screen at Mission Control.

New space sge

The first U.S. space shuttle was launched on April 9, 1981. It was the world's first reusable spacecraft. The shuttle could complete a mission in space, glide back to Earth for a runway landing, and be ready to fly again within 100 working days.
The shuttle was designed as a workhorse, transporting **satellites**, people, and materials into space.

Countdown to Disaster

As *Challenger* exploded, there was a stunned silence at Cape Canaveral. Relatives were at the launch site to watch the lift-off. Including Commander Dick Scobee, there were seven crew members. One was teacher Christa McAuliffe. She was on the shuttle to give lessons from space. None of the crew survived.

This section of the shuttle carries the **payload** and the crew members. It is designed to glide back to Earth at the end of the mission.

1. The cold temperature on January 27 causes concern about the **booster rockets**. At a meeting between **NASA** and Thiokol, the company that built the booster rockets, Thiokol engineers say they have no idea what effect the cold weather will have. One engineer, Roger Boisjoly, warns,"...success of previous flights should not be taken as proof of safety." But the launch is allowed by NASA.

2. Lift-off at 11:38 A.M. The temperature is very cold for Florida—much lower than at any previous launch.

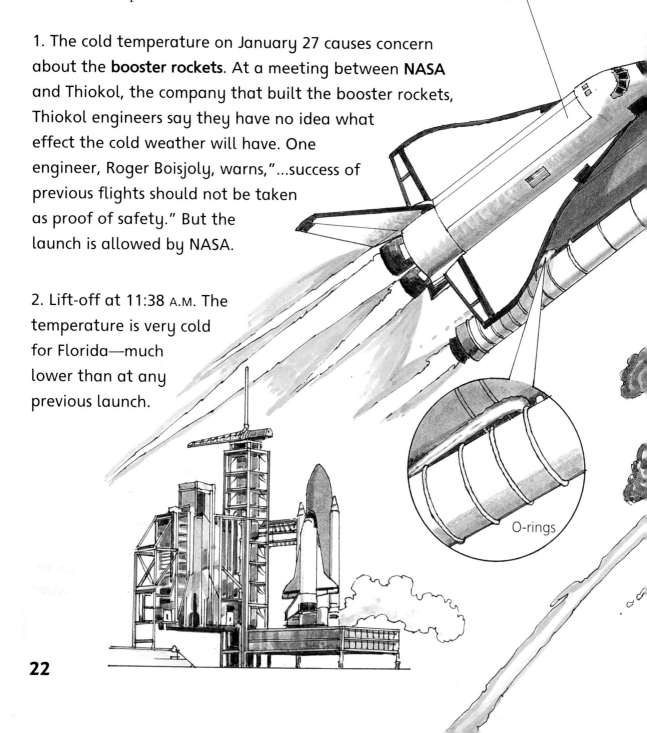

O-rings

In its loadbay, *Challenger* was carrying two **satellites** to put into **orbit**.

tank carrying liquid oxygen and hydrogen fuels

solid fuel booster rockets

7. At 73.13 seconds after lift-off, an explosion totally consumes *Challenger*.

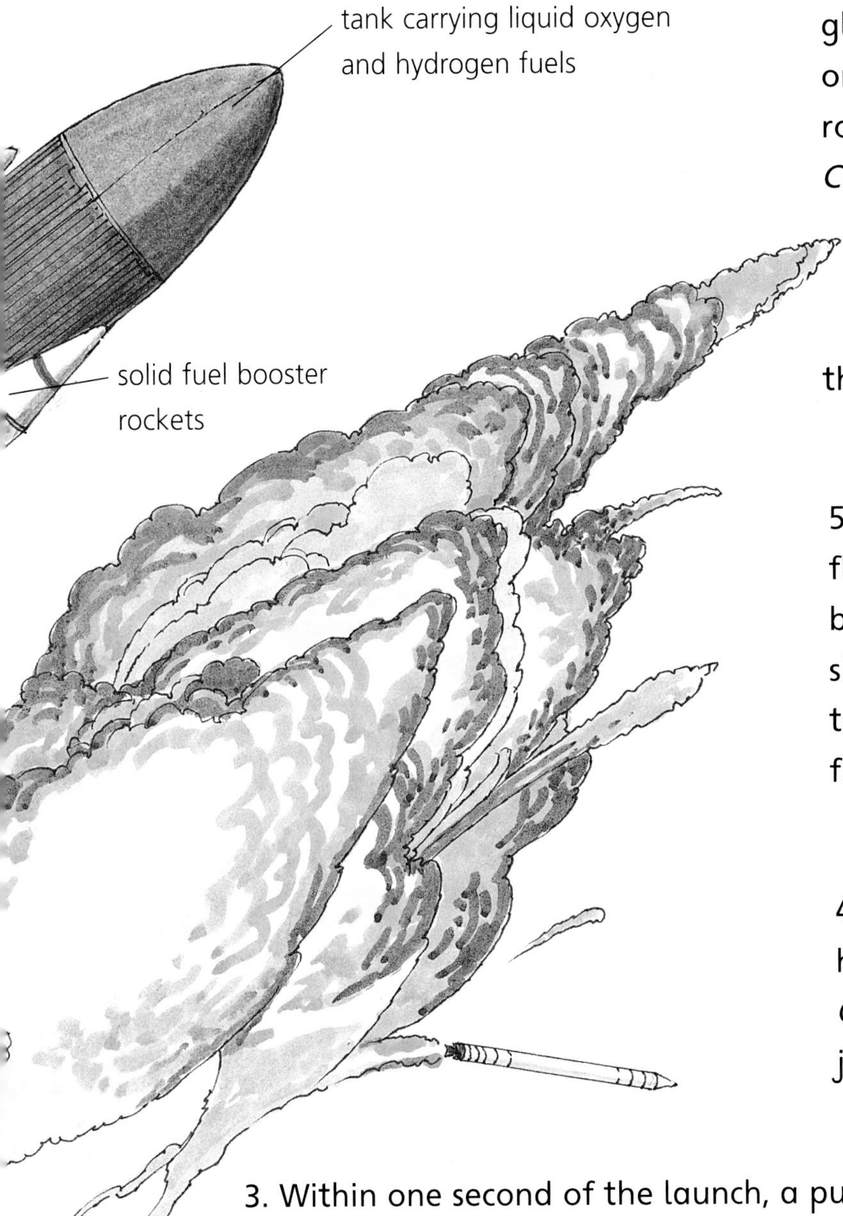

6. By 65 seconds, a bright glowing flame is burning on the side of the booster rocket. At 72 seconds, *Challenger* begins to burn. It is at 45,000 feet (13,800 meters) and traveling at nearly twice the speed of sound.

5. At 59 seconds into the flight, a fire begins to blaze. Pressure readings show that the right-hand tank is losing fuel. The flames are spreading.

4. 37 seconds after lift-off, high winds begin to batter *Challenger*. The weakened joints begin to leak again.

3. Within one second of the launch, a puff of smoke appears from a joint in the right-hand booster rocket. After two and a half seconds, seven more puffs of smoke appear. They are black. It looks like the seal, called an O-ring, in the joint is burning. The burning rubber reseals the leaking joint.

23

The Fatal Mistake

After the *Challenger* disaster, a Presidential Commission was set up to find out what went wrong. A fleet of recovery vessels used **sonar** to search the seabed for the *Challenger*. Wreckage was dredged up, but little trace of the crew members was ever found.

The Presidential Commission made its report in June 1986. It pinpointed the cause of the explosion as the O-rings, which sealed sections of the solid **booster rockets**. But it said the cause of the disaster was the decision made by **NASA** to launch *Challenger* that fateful day. NASA had gone ahead with the launch in spite of the cold weather, and in spite of warnings from engineers who believed that the O-rings were a problem.

Seven crew members lost their lives when *Challenger* exploded.
Front (left to right): Michael Smith, Francis "Dick" Scobee, Ronald McNair.
Back (left to right): Ellison Onizuka, Christa McAuliffe, Gregory Jarvis, Judith Resnik.

O-rings

NASA investigations traced the cause of the explosion to simple rubber seals, called O-rings, between the sections of booster rocket. In each joint there are two O-rings, each less than half an inch thick. These seals were made stiff and hard by the cold weather. Instead of flexing and giving a good seal, they failed. Fuel escaped and burned, and *Challenger* exploded.

Rocket failures

Solid rocket boosters, similar to those on *Challenger*, had been used in nearly 2900 flights for the U.S. space program. 121 of these rockets had failed.

The Presidential Commission found that managers at NASA had taken too many risks. Dr. Feyman of the Commission reported: "The shuttle flies with O-ring erosion and nothing happens. Then it is suggested, therefore, that the risk is no longer so high for the next flights. We can lower our standards a little bit because we got away with it last time. You got away with it but it shouldn't be done over and over again like that."

There were no Shuttle launches for three years after the *Challenger* disaster. The United States had suffered a huge loss.

As part of the *Challenger* inquiry, the O-rings on the future 61-G mission were checked.

The Space Race

Until a few years ago, people often spoke of the "space race." There were only really two runners in the space race—the **USSR** and the U.S. No other countries had the billions of dollars needed to design, build, and launch space rockets.

The USSR and the U.S. competed to be first—first into space, first to do a

spacewalk, and first to the moon. Yet the costs of space exploration were, and are, huge. So there was always a conflict between the engineers and experts who built the space rockets, and the politicians who paid for them. The engineers and experts were cautious, and wanted to have plenty of time to test equipment to make sure it all worked perfectly. Of course, the politicians wanted equipment to work too, but most of all they wanted spectacular successes for their own countries, such as being the first to put a person on the moon.

An american astronaut makes repairs to the Hubble Space Telescope. Until the development of the space shuttle, it was nearly impossible to fix the complex and expensive **satellites** in orbit.

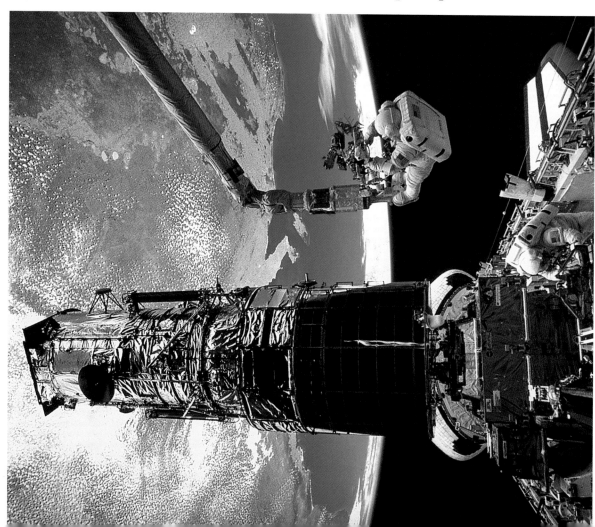

It is important that all satellites are properly tested before they are used.

Most of the time the politicians got the success they wanted. And both the USSR and the U.S. achieved incredible things. Yet sometimes the demand for new successes affected safety and cost lives. The *Challenger* disaster is one example. This was a very important flight for the U.S.

space program. There were 15 more flights planned for that year. Any delay with *Challenger* would have caused problems for the rest of the year. The shuttle program also needed to prove that it was worth all the money it was costing. These pressures meant that when the weather turned cold, and the flight should have been cancelled, it was not.

The World's Worst Space Disasters

There have been over 200 manned space flights. Fortunately, only a few have resulted in disaster.

Baikonur Cosmodrome, Kazakhstan, USSR, October 24, 1960
A rocket preparing for launch explodes on the ground, killing 91 people.

Apollo 13, **April 13, 1970** Sixty hours into the mission to the moon, an explosion disables the **Command Module,** forcing the crew to abandon the mission.

Soyuz 11, **June 29, 1971** The **USSR**'s *Soyuz 11* spacecraft had spent 22 days in space. On **re-entry** into the earth's **atmosphere,** the Command Module loses pressure and the three **cosmonauts** on board are killed.

Challenger, **January 28, 1986** Seven U.S. astronauts are killed when the space shuttle *Challenger* explodes 73 seconds after launch.

This is an artist's impression of the explosion of oxygen tank number one on board *Apollo 13*. The crew never made it to the moon, but they got home safely.

Valentina Tereshkova was the first woman in sapce.

Record breakers

First person in space
In April 1961, Yuri Gagarin of the USSR spent 108 minutes **orbiting** the earth in a spacecraft called *Vostok 1*.

First woman in space
Valentina Tereshkova of the USSR piloted the *Vostok 6* spacecraft in June 1963.

First people to land on the moon
In July 1969 Neil Armstrong and Edwin "Buzz" Aldrin landed the *Apollo 11* **Lunar Module** on the moon.

Longest stay in space
Dr. Valery Polyakov of the USSR spent 438 days on the Russian space station *Mir*. He returned to Earth in March 1995.

Space dangers

Each rocket and the spacecraft it carries contain many hundreds of thousands of separate pieces, from simple seals to complex computers. There are a huge number of things that could go wrong, and sometimes something does. It is almost impossible to build a back-up for every system, so the failure of one small part can destroy a whole mission. All of the disasters in this book were caused by small problems: *Apollo 13* was crippled because of the insulation on some simple wires; the crew of *Soyuz 11* died because of a single **valve**; *Challenger* blew up because of the failure of a seal just millimeters thick. Perhaps it is surprising that there have not been more disasters in space. But as long as there is space travel, the dangers will always be there.

Glossary

air pressure density of the gases in the air

atmosphere envelope of gases which surround the earth

booster rocket large rocket used to get a spacecraft off the ground

combustible capable of burning

Command Module part of the spacecraft where astronauts spend most of their time during a space flight

cosmonaut Russian name for an astronaut

friction force created when one object moves against another

fuel cell cell that makes an electric current from a chemical reaction

fused melted together

GMT (Greenwich Mean Time) time at the Prime Meridian. It is the international standard time.

gravity force which attracts objects to each other and which holds us on the ground

jettisoned dumped or thrown away

launch pad platform used to launch rockets into space

Lunar Module craft that travels to and from the moon

meteorite piece of rock from space

NASA (National Aeronautics and Space Administration) organization in the U.S. that oversees space exploration

orbit oval path through space around a planet or the sun

Orbital Module part of a spacecraft where the astronauts live

payload items carried on board a spacecraft, like satellites

pressure suit suit that protects an astronaut from space, supplying air and heat

pressurized when the inside of a craft is pumped full of air so the astronauts can breathe in the same way as they can on Earth

re-entry when a spacecraft re-enters Earth's atmosphere

retro-fire when engines burn to slow the spacecraft down

satellite object put into space to do tasks such as sending out telephone or television signals, or taking photographs of Earth

Service Module part of a spacecraft that carries equipment

sonar way of finding objects by bouncing sound waves off them

sound barrier high resistance of air to objects approaching the speed of sound

USSR (Union of Soviet Socialist Republics) communist country which included Russia and other nations. It separated in 1991.

space walk when an astronaut leaves the spacecraft in a special suit

Teflon heat-resistant substance developed for use on spacecraft

thermostatic device that controls the temperature of an object

vacuum where there is nothing, not even air

valve device that controls the flow of gas or liquid

venting leaking gas out into space

weightlessness astronauts feel weightless because they cannot feel the effects of gravity in space as they do on Earth

More Books to Read

Gold, Susan D. *To Space & Back: The Story of the Shuttle.* Parsippany, N.J.: Silver Burdett Press, 1992.

Mullane, R. Mike. *Lift Off!: An Astronaut's Dream.* Parsippany, N.J.: Silver Burdett Press, 1994.

Steele, Philip. *Space Travel.* Parsippany, N.J.: Silver Burdett Press, 1991.

Index